Life Stories *is one of those rare books that will touch your soul and perhaps help heal your heart.*

Angela Thomas
Best-selling author and speaker
Author, *Do You Think I'm Beautiful, My Single Mom Life,* and *When Wallflowers Dance*

It is refreshing to see someone with faith handle the delicate subject of death. I pray this book brings healing to a lot of hurt and disappointed people and that it positions them to taste Divine justice.

Bill Johnson
Senior Pastor of Bethel Church in Redding, CA
Author of *When Heaven Invades Earth* and
Face to Face with God

In an era where much of what is published about heartache and sorrow is devoid of any Christian perspective, it is refreshing to encounter a book alive with faith. Ted Hopkins' own acquaintance with sorrow—both personally and professionally—makes this a compelling, hope-filled volume, written in an intimate, conversational style.

Dr. William G. Hoy
President of Grief Resources, Inc.
and editor of *Grief Connections*
Author of *Road to Emmaus: Pastoral Care with the Dying and Bereaved*

Ted Hopkins quickens believers to intimately experience God on a daily basis. His book, an easy read, guides those who want to know how to live in God's Kingdom now. We highly recommend it for those wanting to grow in daily relationship with God.

Al and Betty Lou Bennett
Retired Mercy Ships Captain and Chaplain

I highly recommend Ted's book for families who have lost a loved one through a tragedy or untimely death. God has allowed Ted to experience such tragedy, and he has experienced God's Healing Power. God will truly use this book to help families heal after the loss of a loved one.

R.V. Brown
Evangelist, Author, and Speaker
Director of Outreach to America's Youth, Inc.
Author of *Step Up to the Plate, Dad!*

You will be blessed as you read Ted Hopkins' book, Life Stories, *which reveals the 'language of the heart' in the journey of* Healing and Hope in the Wake of Loss. *Jesus said, 'Follow me and I will make you fishers of men' (Matthew 4:19). Ted obeyed and his journey of following the leading of the Holy Spirit will excite others to examine their hearts to find The Way, The Truth, and The Life in Christ Jesus (John 14:6).*

Rev. Dr. Hilda F. Brittain
Co-Founder of Brittain Ministries, Inc., and
Healing Springs Church, Hickory, NC
Author, *And There is More*

Ted has truly expressed the wonder, power, and reality of the Kingdom of God in this book. We have been brothers in Jesus for over 25 years and his pursuit for all that God has for us here on earth as it is in Heaven has been not only an encouragement to me but also a challenge to be open to the full revelation of the Scriptures through the Holy Spirit. His compassion for others and his integrity in the funeral business have been a bold witness of his faith.

Dr. Larry E. Price, DDS
Dentist in Rose Hill, NC

Only a cheerleader-turned-funeral director could apply his faith to help all of us understand the hope that is available in the midst of despair. Ted has done it again—sacrificing his time so that others might live—really live. This book should be shared with anyone struggling to overcome the loss of a loved one.

Paul Newton
Senior Vice-President, Strategy, Rates, Wholesale
Customers, Commodities, and Analytics
Duke Energy Corporation

As a veteran in the funeral profession, I was extremely encouraged by the way that Ted Hopkins touchingly writes about the stories that so many funeral professionals can tell. I have often heard that being a funeral director is a ministry, and through the stories contained in Life Stories, *Ted proves it.*

Kris Seale
President/CEO of Funeral Directors Life Insurance
Company

Ted Hopkins' heart is quickly evident in the pages of his book, Life Stories. *From cover to cover, it is engaging and it offers thought-provoking insight into the practical application of the Christian life.*

Janet Paschal
Internationally-acclaimed Songwriter, Vocalist,
and Author

LIFE STORIES

Healing *and* Hope in the Wake *of* Loss

TED HOPKINS

DEVELOPMENT SERVICES, INC

Oviedo, Florida

Life Stories: Healing and Hope in the Wake of Loss
by Ted Hopkins

Published by HigherLife Development Services, Inc.
2342 Westminster Terrace
Oviedo, Florida 32765
(407) 563-4806
www.ahigherlife.com

ISBN 13: 978-1-935245-07-0
ISBN 10: 1-935245-07-4

Please note the author has chosen to go against standard grammatical rules and not capitalize the name of satan, therefore, choosing not to give him any recognition.

First Edition
    10 11 12 13 — 8 7 6 5 4 3 2
Printed in the United States of America

DEDICATION

I dedicate this book to my amazing wife April and my three precious daughters, Louisa, Amelia, and Bess. Your thirst for Jesus has opened the door for the Kingdom culture to come, and your passion for life in the Spirit has released the reality of heaven! I am blessed indeed.

CONTENTS

PART ONE:
MY STORY OF HEALING AND HOPE

PART TWO: IN THE KINGDOM OF GOD WE FIND OUR HOPE FOR HEALING

ACKNOWLEDGEMENTS

Fɪʀsᴛ, I ᴡᴀɴᴛ ᴛo thank Carolyn Rutledge for believing in me and encouraging me to complete this project. You are the greatest editor ever!

I also want to thank my "Band of Brothers" who affirmed the word of the Lord on that Tuesday morning when I shared God's calling to write. John, Jim, Penn, and Rick, you guys are awesome. Rick, I especially want to thank you for speaking by faith and declaring the completion of this book. Your encouragement has been a blessing. Dr. Bill Hoy, thank you for the help with the details. Your insight has been invaluable.

Finally, to my mentor and friend, Dr. Larry Price, you have been a radiant beacon of the light for Jesus over the years. Thank you for believing in me and for your faithful friendship. Bless you my friend, my brother.

PREFACE

Call to me and I will answer you and tell you great and
unsearchable things you do not know.

—Jeremiah 33:3

Dr. Nan Preas gave me this Bible verse over 20 years ago
when I considered leaving corporate America. I had never
before received a prophetic word with such confidence from
someone I trust, but, now I find myself working in a family funeral
business and God has called me to write about...*unsearchable
things*...the unsearchable things of human hearts: the hurting
and the hoping. Most importantly, I am a follower of Jesus, and
His profound message of life has led me to this time and this
work.

Thanks to my amazing wife April, I discovered that the Spirit-led
lifestyle is the only solution to walking in victory—walking in His

hope and in His healing. By laying my own agenda aside and becoming more and more intimate with Jesus over the years, the Holy Spirit has begun to reveal His plan and purpose. I marvel at His expectations and intentions because it is clear that, regardless of our status or place in life, we are each created with a Divine Kingdom calling. This book is my response to His call on my life in the work He has given me to do.

I have always been an optimist, regardless of my limitations. How could God possibly call a remedial English student in college and funeral director from Reidsville, North Carolina, to write anything that could impact people from all walks of life? Allow me to answer my own question: I am completely convinced that His unfolding message in the following pages will be words of truth, inspiration, and hope to the multitudes who experience the process of death, loss, and disappointment. With my own personal walk through my brother's suicide as well as the experiences of hundreds of families I have served, the Lord has spoken volumes to me about hurt and hopelessness. Through my experience and His guidance, it is my hope that there will be something of significance and substance for each person who reads these pages, especially for anyone who wonders if their story is beyond God's intervention.

By writing, I feel that I can be completely transparent about my experience of the power of God's Kingdom. Service details and family grief oftentimes interfere with an effort to thoroughly give an account of the hope I have in Christ. I frequently wrestle with the tensions existing between professional limitations and the need to speak into a life which God wants to invade with His Kingdom. My purpose is to add life back into the earthly death equation. If one gets an authentic glimpse that the Kingdom of God is at hand, then the reality of heaven can transform a belief system. God is for us; His righteousness, peace, and joy in the Holy Spirit *will* carry us through tragedy and disappointment.

Offering that message is the purpose of this book, and God is faithful to fulfill His purpose beyond what I can imagine. Pastor Bill Johnson says, "I'm finally figuring out that it is all about Jesus!" These stories are not only about the people involved, and they are certainly not about me. For anyone with "ears to hear," as we read in Mark 4:23 and several other places of Scripture, they are offered as a path to discovering and personally experiencing the Jesus who said, "I have come that they may have life, and have it to the full" (John 10:10b).

First, my own journey is documented as a very personal example of how God has used tragedy, death, and disappointment during my life to bring me into His victory, especially over the last twenty years. What I've come to understand is that *my story* is, in many ways, *our story*—only the details differ. God's intention is to move us into a place of intimacy, obedience, and faith that allows us to see things that we hope for as though they really exist. He is able to make hope and healing a reality for each of us.

The gospel of the Kingdom can be revealed even in the midst of loss and disappointment, and we can discover that abundant life and the reality of heaven *are* still within reach. God has shown me through my experience with families in the darkness of death that the enemy runs full steam ahead with his plans of destruction. As satan interrupts the cycle of life with disease, pain, and tragedy, he can also invade the hearts and minds of survivors with offense, bitterness, and deception.

We often limit our future by our past, but as we step into God's purpose and destiny, He shows us that His plan is for the future and that our stories are tied to *the story*. Jeremiah 29:11 says, "'For I know the plans I have for you,' declares the LORD, 'plans to prosper you and not to harm you, plans to give you hope and a future.'" Each day, we can wake up with a sense of urgency and anticipation that can shake us. What point can there be to waiting any longer to seek and find His purpose, His mercy, His help in time of need?

As we walk together through biblical truths, I will share stories of loss and how the surviving families have embraced the Kingdom to find hope and healing. They have discovered *life* and experienced light beyond the dark places. Some of these stories, at first, might seem to suggest that recovery is overwhelming and impossible, but by the supernatural intervention of His Kingdom, God offers us the chance to see that life, love, and a future have worked together to restore hope and destiny. My prayer is that you will understand that life doesn't end at the grave, nor does it have to wait to begin again at the reunion in heaven.

The calling to offer hope to those who feel lost in a sea of grief and despair brings to mind the mission statement of the United States Air Force Pararescue service:

It is my duty as a Pararescueman to save life and to aid the injured. I will be prepared at all times to perform my assigned duties quickly and efficiently, placing these duties before personal desires and comforts. These things I do, that others may live.

In a very real sense, *Life Stories* tells the tale of our own Guardian, His commitment to placing our needs before Himself, and our opportunity to join Him in spiritual and emotional rescue operations, "that others may live."*

—Ted W. Hopkins
September, 2009

---

* USAF Pararescue motto, originally titled "The Code of the Air Rescueman" and written by Lt. Col. Richard T. Kight. Can be found at http://www.pararescue.com.

There is no agony like bearing an untold story inside of you.*

—Maya Angelou, Poet

* Maya Angelou. Quoted in Avaneda D. Hobbs, *Dr. Maya Angelou: As Seen Through the Eyes of America (Honoring a Woman Full of Life)* (Forestville, Maryland: CAP Publishing & Literary Co. LLC, 1999), page 68.

PART ONE

MY STORY OF HEALING AND HOPE

I'VE AGONIZED OVER THE untold story inside of me, but now I know that it is time! I can relate to Jeremiah 20:9: "But if I say, 'I will not mention him or speak any more in his name,' his word is in my heart like a fire, a fire shut up in my bones. I am weary of holding it in; indeed, I cannot."

The first five chapters of this book tell significant parts of my own story—the experiences God has walked me through to get me to this point of writing this book. May He be glorified in the telling.

Chapter 1

FAMILY, PERSONAL LOSS, REDEMPTION

I WILL NEVER FORGET JUNE 28, 1977—I was only 16 years old. The first and best thing that happened to me was to be born to Norman and Preston Hopkins, or Hop and Pep as my father and mother are affectionately called. I had an amazing childhood! There were three of us children: Tim, Tami, and Ted. We had a very normal family and were blessed in every way. We were neither wealthy nor poor. Dad and Mom did everything possible to make our house a home. Going on family camping trips, working in the garden, helping with the chores, singing around the piano, having plenty of good food—these are the fondest memories of my family.

Hard work was expected. It always seemed like we raised enough vegetables to feed the entire town, but it was only enough for our family, extended family, and a few neighbors. We had cows and chickens, and I clearly remember Mom's churning butter. Dad and Mom taught us the value of a dollar and the importance of working together as a team. Our little farm was a schoolyard for discipline, responsibility, and even the facts of life.

Teamwork and careful attention to chores always paid off. We often went fishing with Dad and had lots of playtime in the woods and at the creek. The song "Boondocks," by Little Big Town sums up well my memories of home: "...a tin roof, a front porch and a gravel road... You get a line, I'll get a pole, we'll go fishin' in a craw fish hole...."*

Beyond work at home, Dad was a diligent provider who worked the necessary hours at the local textile mill, while Mom stayed home during our early years and later worked at the local Department of Social Services. Their marriage was a true picture of love and partnership. I remember them agreeing on almost

---

* Words and Music by WAYNE KILPATRICK, KIMBERLY ROADS, PHILLIP SWEET, KAREN FAIRCHILD CHILDERS, and JIMI WESTBROOK. © 2003 WARNER-TAMERLANE PUBLISHING CORP., SELL THE COW MUSIC, TOWER ONE MUSIC, WB MUSIC CORP. and TOWER TWO, a Division of BLA PUBLISHING. All rights on Behalf of itself, SELL THE COW MUSIC and TOWER ONE MUSIC Administered by WARNER-TAMERLANE PUBLISHING CORP. All rights reserved. Used by permission.

everything. We always felt secure with our parents' love for each other and their commitment to the Lord.

One of the keenest memories of growing up in the Hopkins' house was that we *always* went to church: twice on Sunday, once on Wednesday night, and any other time something special was going on. There was one thing for sure: it wasn't just show! My parents truly were godly people. They were, and still are, servants in the greatest sense of the word. If anyone needed anything, most folks knew that a call to Hop and Pep would mean that help was on its way. They lived their faith out loud and led us in the goodness of God. Honor, truth, and integrity were the standard, and it would prove to be the stronghold for the storm yet to come.

Tim, the oldest, struggled with self-esteem and often wrestled with finding his place. As a child, Tim was genteel, kind, and gracious. He never wanted to cause trouble for anyone. Even though his disposition was sweet, his physical presence was misleading. He matured quickly and was much taller and larger than most of the kids in his class. He was often thrown in with the older boys and always felt pressured to measure up to his older peers. Dad said that Tim was gifted with great balance and athleticism, though Tim never excelled in sports. He was very musical, both vocally and instrumentally, but he really never had the opportunity to shine as a musician. The four-year difference in our ages makes it difficult for me to verbalize my early recollections of Tim, but I have many memories from his middle school years and later.

During those middle school years, Tim became very intrigued with God. After he made the decision to follow Jesus, he had many questions about the deeper things of God. Because of his youth, I'm convinced that he may have been a bit intimidating with his zeal and hunger for the Kingdom. He was passionate about his faith and wondered why others in the church didn't feel the same. He was hungry for the gifts of the Spirit but felt squelched by the doctrine of the church and the apathy of the deacons. I believe that he was misunderstood by church folks and, unfortunately, turned to the world, believing the lie that it had a better solution to the mysteries of life.

From the time he entered high school, Tim began to choose death by virtue of his friendships and activities. He always tried to make up for being younger by willingly taking dares from his so-called friends. Older kids laughed at his attempts to fit in, and Tim used the laughter to validate the acceptance of his peers. Peer pressure quickly took over his life. Many of his friends smoked, and he started there. He tried alcohol and drugs, which led to deep addictions and the need for cash. He made connections and became a supplier. Everything that was contrary to our home became his obsession. He loved music, and rock music quickly became his new passion. It led him down the path of rebellion, sex, and whatever felt good. The deception that guided Tim in his allegiance to the false authority is the very deception that made him question his own self-worth. My heart breaks to write these words, but this testimony is part of the truth that leads to life.

As a seventh grader, I was chosen to have a role in the high school production of *The Music Man* and was forced to enter Tim's world of deception. We spent a lot of time together, and it was then that I discovered he was doing things that I would have never expected from *our* family. I knew our parents' expectations, and the standard was truth and right decisions.

In the midst of my new discovery, I stepped into deep friendship with my big brother. He trusted me and would wake me on many late night arrivals home and pour out his soul. I listened but didn't have a clue what to do. He confided in me, and it was way bigger than anything I could handle at that time in my life. Because of the darkness in his life, fear defined my response. I would *not* tell on him because of the unknown, and I knew that I couldn't "rat" on him.

Most importantly during this time together, I began to see that I did *not* want to follow his lead. He could see my reservations, and he even claimed that I would fall. He said that I would both drink my first beer and have sex before leaving high school. I looked straight in his eyes and promised that I would not, and, by the grace of God, I stayed firm on those convictions.

As Tim made his way through high school, he struggled with his place. Finally, after his graduation, he got some devastating news. He thought that his girlfriend was pregnant, and his world crashed in on him. All of his bad choices began to surface, and he was confronted with the decision for Christ made back in middle school. He had received forgiveness but had become overwhelmed with the mess he had made. He knew that he had fallen off of the path of God's plan and purpose for his life. Even though God stood with his arms open wide, Tim never forgave himself. He was broken, and satan had completely hidden the message of the Redeemer. He suffered a nervous breakdown and never recovered from that hard fall. Those first few days were awful. I remember his weeping and pleading for forgiveness. His habits affected him emotionally and spiritually, but his heavy drug abuse crushed him physically. He was very sick for over a year and a half.

Our family pulled together, trying everything we knew to bring hope and healing. We tried medical and psychological care, yet every attempt was unproductive. The next year and a half seemed hopeless for Tim. He felt trapped and worthless. From his perspective, life had nothing to offer and his only option was to believe and embrace satan's lie. My parents were in a desperate search and finally discovered a faith-based institution just right for Tim's situation. He was accepted, and we felt that his future was bright.

June 28, 1977, began with sunshine and optimism as we prepared for Tim to leave but ended as one of our darkest days as a family. Mom was planning to take Tim, while Dad and I were scheduled to go out of town to help my uncle move. There were a few items that Tim needed for the trip, so Mom made a quick run to town. She was gone for about one hour. Most people who live on the farm hunt and fish, and they usually keep guns close for whatever reason. Dad had taken all but one of the guns out of the house because of Tim's fragile condition. That one was hidden, but, as far as I'm concerned, the suicide demon revealed that gun to my brother in that moment of seclusion, and Tim responded to that lying spirit by taking his own life. This tragic invasion by the enemy was devastating, but, in hindsight, I can see that this day marked the beginning of a deeper understanding of restoration and hope.

We are not sure when Tim discovered the gun, but when he found it, he went with it to one of our barns, and upon Mom's return, she walked into darkness, silence, and fear. Frantically, she called for Tim. There was no response. She found her way to the barn, and, after discovering his lifeless body, she stumbled to the house and somehow found the wits to call a dear neighbor. Help came from all directions. It was a horrific day.

Not yet aware of the tragedy, Dad and I returned home. There was an entourage of folks waiting to catch us. Our pastor and some of the men of the church felt that it would be better to warn us before arriving at home with all of the turmoil and extra cars at the house. As a 16-year-old, this was my first experience with personal tragedy and loss. I was broken for my mom and dad; I felt helpless. I wanted, somehow, to fix this injustice.

That night, I was determined to get answers. I was desperate to hear from God, and I wanted to know how and why this could happen to a family like ours. How could this suicide invade our household with such boldness? We were striving to find answers and this happened. The nightmare became real and the enemy's purpose was fulfilled with the death of my brother. Out of the darkness, God's love entered that room, and He spoke these words to me, "Don't ask Me why. Ask, 'How can I handle this?' Tim was deceived. I love him, and he is forgiven." Words of hope and life.

This was my first authentic encounter with Jesus. I was changed forever.

Looking back, I recognize that occasion as the worst day and the best day of my life. Let me explain. I know now that God's Holy Spirit revealed Himself to me as the One that Jesus spoke about in John 14:26-27:

> But the Counselor, the Holy Spirit, whom the Father will send in my name, will teach you all things and will remind you of everything I have said to you. Peace I leave with you; my peace I give you. I do not give to you as the world gives. Do not let your hearts be troubled and do not be afraid.

Fear left and the Shalom of heaven carried me through the night!

My brother's death established a benchmark of my commitment to Jesus. He loved me in the darkest hour, and I discovered the reality of His presence. It established a hunger and thirst for God that convinced me that there was more to the gospel than just words and sermons. Even though God seemed to correct my first question, I knew without hesitation that He loved me. I knew that He had plans for me and that Jesus was absolutely real. It was eternally clear that He would never leave me nor forsake me. I spoke verbally that night to the Lord and said, "I will follow You. I will trust You, and I will open my heart for You to speak life and hope to me, even in the midst of this storm." I promised that I would *not* be a victim of peer pressure and that I would lean on Him to make right decisions and do my best to live up to the standard my parents had set before me.

In that hour, God understood my innocence and desperation, and He wrapped me in his amazing arms of love. His supernatural presence overwhelmed me and affirmed that He would lead me into His plan and purpose. In darkness, there was light!

CHAPTER 2

DISCOVERING THE PATH OF GOD'S PURPOSE

M Y WITNESS TO GOD's gifts of hope and healing moves forward with more information about my family, especially my sister, Tami, and the spiritual journey God had for me to take. Tami was a pleaser, the ideal daughter who helped Mom around the house and did everything she could to be compliant and obedient. She was popular, talented, and successful—the chief junior marshal, head cheerleader, homecoming queen, and accompanist for the glee club. Beyond all of her accolades, she was real, and I thought she was the greatest. For whatever reason, her praise of my success meant the most to me. We were best friends all through high school, and our relationship grew even deeper through the family tragedy.

Needless to say, Mom and Dad were devastated, and they needed stability, compliance, and obedience, so Tami and I did everything we could to settle the turmoil in our household. I decided to pour myself into anything positive and productive for my future including music, sports, and the books. I wanted to make right choices in things that were honorable and true so that my parents wouldn't have to worry. I certainly didn't do everything right, but God did protect me from most wrong decisions, and Mom and Dad slept at night.

Tami worried about Tim even as a little girl. She followed him around for fear of his being left out or something going wrong. She had been away at college during that last year of Tim's life and was very concerned for our family. Her 1977 summer teaching job involved tutoring children around the county. On the day of Tim's death, she had the feeling that something was going to happen. She made her way home early to find the confusion and tragedy of the suicide. With strength and courage, she stepped in, brought stability, and carried us through the funeral that difficult summer and the difficult years that followed.

Tami's leadership helped to define my direction, and I moved forward with hope and my usual optimism. I've never forgotten Zig Ziglar's description of optimism from his popular tape series, "See You At the Top": "I'm the type that would go fishing for Moby Dick in a row boat and take the tartar sauce." The sun was and is always shining in my world, and, even after Tim's death, I chose to live every day to the fullest. I agreed with the word Jesus spoke to me the night of Tim's death and sought my purpose and destiny full throttle. I camped on my life Bible verse, Philippians 4:8: "Finally, brothers, whatever is true, whatever is noble, whatever is right, whatever is pure, whatever is lovely, whatever is admirable—if anything is excellent or praiseworthy—think about such things."

Favor went before me, and I had teachers who made me believe I could accomplish anything. Duane Best, Bill Carter, Teresa Price, Wayne Barker, and many others encouraged me to expect excellence and success. I also had one bosom friend, Paul Newton. We believed in each other and stood together throughout high school and college. To this day, he is my brother and remains one of my closest friends. I believed them and achieved success in academics, athletics, and student leadership. The door opened for me to be accepted at the University of North Carolina (UNC) at Chapel Hill, and the opportunities continued. I made the junior varsity cheer squad my freshman year and cheered the next three years on the varsity squad. What a dream come true!! During my time cheering, we won the ACC football championship, three football bowl championships, two trips to the final four basketball championships, and, finally, I served as co-captain my senior year in 1982—the national championship season with Michael Jordan, James Worthy, and crew. It was an honor to work with one of the greatest coaches in college basketball history, Coach Dean Smith. He treated us as part of the team and made it his business to call

me by name whenever we crossed paths. These are memories I'll cherish forever.

After graduation from UNC, I landed a sales management position with one of the top consumer goods companies in the world: Proctor and Gamble. The experience and training that I received from P&G was an invaluable time of personal development and maturity. It clearly established my confidence with business and management.

During this period of success and growth, my sister told me about this beautiful girl with whom she taught. She told me not to ask questions; I just had to meet her. I despised blind dates, but I trusted Tami. From the first glance, I was smitten. April was amazingly fun, clever, and confident. It was obvious that she was beautiful, but the most intriguing thing was her relationship with Jesus. She had an understanding about the gospel that was completely foreign to me. She seemed to know Jesus so intimately; it was as if He was standing right there with her. I had *never* met anyone like that before. We would share and pray together, though my prayers came out very sterile and "churchy." Then she would take over, making me feel like Jesus would "show up," and our prayer time would come alive. There was power and confidence in every word with full anticipation that God was hearing and answering her prayers. I knew that this lady had something that I needed. I fell head over heels in love with her, and I needed her to walk with me to find God's destiny and purpose. It was obvious that something was missing, and I felt that it had something to do with the encounter I had had with Jesus the night of Tim's death.

I had met charismatic Christians and "Spirit-filled" people before that time, but they always seemed overly confident and condescending. April was never arrogant about her faith. She was never condemning toward me, and her unconditional love was contagious. As our relationship grew, April's walk with Jesus fueled my appetite for the deeper things of God. I chased April and Jesus right to the altar. We were married, moved to Richmond, Virginia, and landed in an amazing Presbyterian Church. When we first arrived, the preacher was teaching on the gifts of the Spirit, revealing truths such as, "It's not how much of the Spirit you have, but how much the Spirit has of you." Unfortunately, the only thing I knew about the Holy Spirit was that He was part of the Trinity. I did not understand His purpose and the life He brings to the believer.

Every person we met at St. Giles had a spirit much like April's. It was the most exciting church environment I had ever experienced. On one of our early visits, we met an older couple who almost "bubbled" up to us. They were "dripping" with Jesus, and there was a genuine love and acceptance that gave us a sense of security. Jenny and John Van Norden became our Richmond parents and spiritual mentors. They had moved from St. Paul's Episcopal Church in Darien, Connecticut, with one of the finest Bible teachers in the world, Reverend Dr. Everett "Terry" Fullam.

As we shared, the Van Nordens opened their magnificent tape library of Bible teachings. I listened to personal testimonies of people who had been to church for years, and I finally discovered the "more" God intended for me and the joy the Bible

communicates. As I studied with Terry Fullam's teachings, I was convinced that he had the Bible memorized. The Holy Spirit became my teacher, and the Bible came to life. Every time I opened the Word or listened to teachings, it was like the Fourth of July. Every day was a celebration, and my friendship with Jesus grew.

One particular series of Terry's sermons was life-changing for me. He taught on the Holy Spirit, and it opened the fullness of the Kingdom that validated my search. My Southern Baptist background had me scared to death of "Charismaniacs" speaking in tongues and swinging from chandeliers. But as I listened to this brilliant teacher explain the Bible, and as I allowed the Holy Spirit freedom within, Jesus became my passion. I came to better understand the dynamic truth of Matthew 3:11, the passage in which John the Baptist says, "I baptize you with water for repentance. But after me will come one who is more powerful than I, whose sandals I am not fit to carry. He will baptize you with the Holy Spirit and with fire."

I read the Bible, listened to tapes, asked questions, and prayed for over two years before the baptism of the Holy Spirit became a reality. It's important to make it clear that, while I had received Jesus as my savior early in my life, it was clear that I did not understand the "fire" or "power" parts, as in Acts 1:8 when Jesus says, "You will receive power...."

I knew that there had to be more than just words and sermons, and I was convinced that when Jesus said, "I have come that they may have life" (John 10:10), it was not just something to say but something to become! Finally, one night when April was away from home, I decided to give Jesus everything and allow Him to be my Lord, and He came and dunked me with His Spirit. I realized that my cup had never been full. From that point, it became like an artesian well. Terry Fullam used to put it this way: "No longer will a little dab do you." As Jesus baptized me with His Spirit, I realized He loved me more than I had ever known. I was in awe of His presence, and I walked around the house weeping and worshiping the King. In those moments, He was wrapping me up with the gift of the Holy Spirit, and I fell even more deeply in love with Jesus. After that, He was all I could think about. I thought I was hungry before, but now I understood my obsession.

In the spring of 1987, I went with my dear friend Dr. Larry Price, my father-in-law, Bob Wilkerson, my brother-in-law Mark Wilkerson, and a few others to a Christian Believers' United Men's Conference in Montreat, North Carolina, entitled, "Rise Up Oh Men of God." I was shaken to the core! I had never seen a group of men in such unity and completely sold out for Jesus. The teachings that weekend were foundational for me as God began to speak to me about His plan and purpose for my future. After my Holy Spirit awakening, it was as though I saw God and heard His voice at every turn, and these Spirit-filled men spoke His word with power and conviction. It was obvious to me that they didn't just know the words, but they *believed them.* The words were full of life, and it was time for *me* to rise up. God was calling me to trust Him in *all* things, and it was apparent that change was coming.

~ Chapter 3 ~

FUNERAL SERVICE?!

T HE MESSAGES OF THE men's conference reached the deepest fiber of my soul, and I knew God was stirring me to address my anxiety with corporate America. Proctor and Gamble had everything I could hope for by the world's standard, including financial security and corporate advancement. But I felt like a bird in a cage. I felt trapped, and it took a Spirit-filled weekend in the mountains of North Carolina to show me that it was time to trust God with the next step. It was with a bunch of men sold out for Jesus and the life-breathing words, "Rise up, young man of God!" that released me to consider change. Dr. Morris Sheets challenged us to "be a Daniel" and to live and operate with divine courage. I wasn't sure what that meant, but I knew that he was talking to me, and, as far as I was concerned, it was a word straight from God.

Six months later, April and I decided to leave the P&G safety net and to step out, trusting that God would carry us into the unknown. I remembered one of the sermons by Terry Fullam entitled, "Life on Wings." This was a word calling believers to be "Eagle Christians." Eagles do not grovel on the ground; they mount up with power and soar on the winds with anticipation and hope. Eagle Christians watch for the winds of the Spirit and let go with the anticipation that God will meet them in that place of faith and hope. In the same sermon, Dr. Fullam gave a wonderful paraphrase of God's call for Abraham to leave his home:

> Being a person of great influence, there was probably a huge send off. All of the dignitaries of Ur would have been there, no doubt. At some point, someone would have come up to him and said, "Abram, we're going to miss you, by the way, where are you going?"
>
> And of course Abram says, "Well, um...uh...it's not all that easy to say. As a matter of fact, I really don't know."
>
> "You don't know where you are going? Well, then how will you know when you get there?"
>
> "God will tell me!"
>
> "God will tell you. Abram you are a fool! Are you going to leave your family and everything you have and follow a God you can't even see?"
>
> And I can imagine Abram saying, "Yes, that's exactly what I'm going to do."
>
> Let me say something to you, if you decide that you are going to be serious about walking with God, don't expect the encouragement of the world. And

unfortunately, many times even the church will not encourage you.[*]

Our own journey involved a move from our familiar surroundings. We left for Rockingham County, home of both the Hopkins and the Wilkerson families. I started in financial services, and for almost three years I muddled through selling life insurance, mutual funds, and tangible investments. It was a grueling, difficult time for April and me. We wandered for a season that seemed like an eternity. We suffered financially and wondered if God was going to show us His plan and purpose. The one belief that we both agreed on was that God had spoken clearly that He wanted us to make family a priority. Our first daughter, Louisa, was born, and April had to go back to work. She stood by me, believing that God would not leave or forsake us. She was so faithful, and I have always cherished her trust and confidence.

I was questioning whether I had missed God completely and decided to network with every smart, successful businessman I knew. It is amazing how some things can be right in front of our noses, and yet we look right past the obvious. Once again, favor went before me as local executives and professionals opened their doors to me for advice. I'll never forget the words of one of the most successful philanthropists of our area, Mr. Dalton McMichael, who said, "Didn't you marry one of the Wilkerson girls? You must have talked to Pitt about that funeral parlor over

---

[*] Dr. Terry Fullam, "Life on Wings" (sermon, Holy Spirit Conference, November 10-12, 1989).

in Reidsville. Seems to me that the funeral business would fit you to a tee." Of course, my first thought was, "You must be crazy. A funeral director?"

God fanned the idea! Maybe, somehow, my brother's death *could* be used for good. April and I talked, we communicated with her parents, and we finally talked with her grandfather, Mr. Pitt Wilkerson. We looked carefully at the possibilities, and God made it clear that funeral service was intended for my future. On June 20, 1990, I found myself sitting at a small cluttered desk, not far from Mr. Wilkerson, with a new job at the funeral home.

The Wilkerson firm was a three-generation family business, established in 1909 by William Henry Wilkerson, April's great-grandfather. His sons, Robert and Pittman, joined the operation during the 1930s and continued serving the Rockingham County community over the next fifty years. Robert (Bobby) L. Wilkerson, April's father, joined the firm in the 1950s. During the 1980s, Pittman, "Mr. Pitt," continued to operate the business as he had over the past generations, and it was obviously time for change. When I joined the Wilkersons, Bobby was ready to move forward, and he embraced every idea with openness and excitement. My corporate experience and even the time I spent in financial services both proved invaluable. I knew nothing about the funeral business, but God blessed us with supernatural insight, wisdom, and favor. After only a very few short months, April's sister, Drew, joined the business. With her accounting background and attention to detail, we knew that she was a gift from God! The miracles happened almost daily. God's timing was perfect! We all had different gifts and were able to implement subtle changes in the operations that successfully improved every aspect of our service.

Throughout my early days working with the family, it was apparent that funeral service was more than business. If I have said it once, I have said it a thousand times, "The one thing that the Wilkersons know how to do is to love the families they serve." We all agreed that if families were willing to trust us to care for their loved ones, genuine care and service had to be our priority. I asked my father-in-law, considering his lifetime in the family business, "What is the most important thing in funeral service?" I will never forget his answer! Without hesitation, he said, "There are three things: service, service, and service." We made that our philosophy in every decision, and I could see the hand of God moving me into His plan and purpose.

As I began to understand the pulse of the business, it became obvious that funeral service provided the perfect professional environment that would foster both business and ministry. I realized that I needed to get my funeral director's license, so I served my apprenticeship and completed the necessary schooling requirements.

Right away, I could see that my gifting worked well in that environment. It was a natural fit for my personality, and, very early on, I felt comfortable dealing with the delicate needs of families experiencing grief and loss. As I began waiting on families, I knew that I had to maintain a professional approach to the business at hand, but it was also clear that I had to allow my personal relationship with Jesus to guide me through each family's loss. The proper balance was critical in keeping my perspective on the practical needs of the business. At the same time, my heart led me to continue pursuing my personal hunger and thirst for God.

Over the next ten years, God honored and blessed our efforts at the funeral home. Even though I was not a Wilkerson, I was warmly received by the community and was welcomed by the longtime friends of the family. The operations improved consistently each year. As we updated our facilities and equipment, the Lord also began to help us build an amazing staff and team that embraced our vision and purpose. I am so proud of the people who work so hard each day to make the Wilkerson service the best it can be. The previous generations of service laid the foundation for us to restore confidence as we made consistent and positive changes to the business.

Throughout this time, ministry opportunities surfaced at work and in the community. Every day I felt more comfortable bringing the Kingdom of God into the equation with the families I was serving. At the same time, I was finding favor with the pastors and churches of the county. April and I were very concerned about the youth culture and felt led to pray for a solution. Within weeks, our precious friends Jenny and John Van Norden invited us to experience The Gathering Place. This is a ministry in St. Simons Island, Georgia, that has had a radical impact for the Kingdom. We rallied parents, pastors, and youth leaders, and God miraculously opened the door for a county-wide youth ministry. The Gathering Place of Rockingham County reached across denominational and cultural boundaries and touched the lives of hundreds of youth and adults. It was obvious that my passion for Jesus could be used in both places.

After The Gathering Place season, I again questioned my specific purpose and direction. Was God calling me to business or ministry? My position at the funeral home had developed into a role of leadership and responsibility, and I was beginning to feel the common funeral service burnout. I knew that I could not simply spend my days waiting for someone to die; there had to be something more.

In the late '90s, we were still operating in the same facility that the Wilkersons moved into in 1947. The facility limited us in every way. I was starting to feel frustrated and confined and very unsure about our future. I desperately needed to hear from God. April and I had been blessed with three beautiful daughters, and we both knew that we needed clarity for the next chapter of our life story.

Out of the blue, we were invited to a Focus on the Family ministry update event in Greensboro, North Carolina. There was nothing special about the meeting other than the fact that God used this event to speak into our future. Kurt Leander was the presenter, and we were instantly drawn to each other. Through an unusual course of events, Focus approached April and me to consider joining the ministry of Focus on the Family. We were overwhelmed and forced to take a hard look at the opportunity. The girls packed and flew with us to Colorado Springs for the interviews. Our time with the Focus family was amazing. The Public Affairs team made a unanimous offer. Mac McQuiston made one comment, though, that hit home. He said, "I think that you are the perfect match for this position, but I believe in my heart that there's some music yet to be played in funeral service for you." Music has always been an important part of my life, and with the music analogy, along with the unfinished resolve I was feeling inside, God let me know that He had something more for me at home in the funeral business.

The fresh Spirit of God had breathed life into our future, and within just a few short months, we completed plans to build a new funeral home facility. A groundbreaking ceremony turned the page for the next amazing chapter for the Hopkins family and Wilkerson Funeral Home.

~ CHAPTER 4 ~

THE NEXT CHAPTER...

...those who hope in the Lord will renew their strength. They will soar on wings like eagles; they will run and not grow weary, they will walk and not be faint.

—Isaiah 40:31

Jᴏʜɴ Eʟᴅʀᴇᴅɢᴇ'ꜱ ʙᴏᴏᴋ *Epic: The Story God Is Telling* and Eldredge's intimate, heartfelt presentation at the Catalyst conference in the fall of 2004 set me on course to get a glimpse into what he called *story*.* Just like the words Sam spoke to Frodo in *The Fellowship of the Ring*, "I wonder what sort of tale we've

---

* John Eldredge, *Epic: The Story God is Telling* (Nashville: Thomas Nelson, 2007).

wandered into?", Eldredge created an atmosphere of wonder for me as well.* From his first breath, I found myself enamored with the idea that *my story* was indeed intended from the creation of the world to play a part in *the story*. This passionate pursuit I have felt in my spirit was not just a passing fancy but clearly a full-blown, God-planted purpose and destiny. Eldredge described *story* as the language of the heart, which includes love, adventure, romance, and the battle between good and evil. It was amazing to see that my story had been intentional.

My hunger for Jesus had landed me right in the middle of the greatest epic ever told. My life was wrapped around relationships at home, at work, and at play. I had built all that I am and ever intend to be around others. A villain appeared in my story at every turn. I could see that even in the midst of success and break-through, satan never rested in his interference. It was obvious that I was clearly in a battle for my children and my family. Finally, I realized that I was in a battle against the villain and his invasion for the lives of the families whom I was serving every day at work. Like in every good story, there has to be a rescue, and I was called to somehow step into that position. Allow me to go back and explain how God developed my story to lead me toward that role.

---

* J.R.R. Tolkien, *The Fellowship of the Ring* Copyright © 1954, 1965, 1966 by J.R.R. Tolkien; 1954 edition copyright ©renewed 1982 by Christopher R. Tolkien, Michael H.R. Tolkien, John F.R. Tolkien and Priscilla M.A.R. Tolkien; 1965/1966 editions copyright © renewed 1993, 1994 by Christopher R. Tolkien, John F.R. Tolkien and Priscilla M.A.A. Tolkien.

The anxious days were commonplace during the construction project, but each moment was filled with excitement and anticipation. My brother-in-law, Don McGee, worked closely with my father-in-law on the landscaping and the visual imagery of the exterior of the property, while my mother-in-law, Flo, used her amazing eye and interior design prowess to decorate the interior with precision. My sister-in-law, Drew, is so clever and was helpful with the details both inside and out. It was an amazing time of unity and teamwork for the family.

Looking back over the previous ninety years of the funeral service, we were keenly aware that the move involved a difficult transition. Even though the old funeral home limited our capacity, we had to consider the history of the business and the thousands of families who had found refuge in that old building. There was over half a century of memories and funeral services etched into the minds of families from all over Rockingham County. Family events like weddings and funerals often serve as benchmarks, whether it is the excitement of a new tomorrow or the uncertainty of transition and loss. Keeping this in mind, it was critical that we maintain the "down home" atmosphere as well as the personalized approach to each family we served.

As we settled into the new facility, we marveled at the opportunities that lay ahead for the funeral home. The new location established our progressive approach and affirmed our commitment to quality care and the future of funeral service. I continued to look inside to hear God's call for my life. Reflecting back over my time at the funeral home, I could see that the many different circumstances of the first decade helped to define my identity and to bring clarity to my purpose. I was finding my place as father and husband, I was sorting through my role in community service and ministry, and I was gaining a better understanding of my responsibilities at work. It was apparent that God was developing my strengths and bringing clarity to His plans for my future.

During the early stages of our local youth ministry days, Randy Bruno, the executive director of The Gathering Place on St. Simons Island, called me a visionary. In biblical terms, he described God's blessing in my life as an "apostolic gift." It was a true word of encouragement for me, and that gift has continued to grow and mature. Not only do I see the trees, but I also see the forest. I am always looking for new ideas and striving for excellence. My competitive spirit can be both a blessing and a curse. I sometimes drive everyone crazy with my plans to improve or embellish the services which we already provide. The sky was the limit at the new facility, but no matter how things improved with the business, I continued to feel that God was calling me to dig deeper into Kingdom living and His eternal purpose.

The most exciting aspect about this journey with Jesus is that the Word is always fresh, and it is not about what He did yesterday but what He *is* doing and the anticipation of what He is *going to do* tomorrow. In the same way, the Bible says that "faith comes from hearing" not from having heard (Rom. 10:17). Daily we get to search out the heart of God and discover the peace of God that passes understanding. Like Dr. Fullam said to me and others many times, "People often ask, how do you know God's will and find the peace of God? It is clear that the peace of God that passes understanding reveals itself when you walk in the path of God's purpose for you." It is so true; walking in the path of God's purpose is, without doubt, the most exciting way to live.

As the calendar rolled over to the 21st century, there was a lot more happening in my life beyond the changes at the funeral home. The path of God's purpose broadened each day. Our family life was blooming in every field. We had the opportunity to build and to move into our new home. The girls, Louisa, Amelia, and Bess, embraced our love for Jesus, and the Kingdom of God became the guide to our plans and purposes as a family. At every turn, the girls were finding success—the classroom, music, and theatre. Every day was an adventure, and we were enjoying the ride. Music was the main thread for the family. Early on, the girls sang at nursing homes as a part of Christmas giving, and as they discovered harmonies, their gifts developed and amazing doors opened. They even had the opportunity to sing the national anthem for the Atlanta Braves!

During this same period of time, the Van Nordens introduced me to the ministry of Bethel Church and Pastor Bill Johnson. We often get distracted with the activity of life and lose focus on our true love, so his ministry served as a feeding ground for my soul. Pastor Bill awakened that voracious appetite for the Word, and I was constantly hungry and thirsty. As he often says, it was clear that the Holy Spirit in me wanted out! I was hearing about a culture that lived by faith, anticipating that God was anxious to show up in every circumstance. The thirst within me became a river of hope, and, as it spilled over, I had to give it to anyone who would listen.

While He was feeding my soul, God was opening the door for several close personal friendships. We met John Waller and his precious wife, Tina, one Sunday morning, and they quickly became close friends. John and I started meeting once a week, praying over each other and seeking God. The Holy Spirit would meet us there, and I witnessed the miraculous hand of God move in John's life. The truth is just as John 7:37b-38 says: "If anyone is thirsty, let him come to me and drink. Whoever believes in me, as the Scripture has said, streams of living water will flow from within him." That well of living water was released, and John overflows with God's truth wherever he goes.

Soon after John and I started our weekly time with the Lord, God entrusted me to reach out to other men as well. It was an interesting season because I never really saw myself as the one-on-one type. Nonetheless, it was a very natural, fulfilling time, and our meetings grew from two men to five. There were other men who were calling for counsel, and I found myself ministering to other men as well.

Throughout this period of time, once again, I began to question the focus of my calling. I knew God was using me at the funeral home with families, and it was also apparent that the men were growing and stepping into the Kingdom lifestyle. All the while, I was desperate to find my purpose and discover if *my* story really mattered. Was there anything more in the grand scheme of

God's eternal plan, beyond the daily responsibilities at Wilkerson Funeral Home?

Beyond my experiences of loss and disappointment, what would I do next? How could I bring the and-they-lived-happily-ever-after element to the story of my life? I could see it on the personal side with family and friends, but how would I bring life and hope to the funeral parlor? My prayer became, "God, I'm willing, and I'm running to Your arms for vision and understanding. Teach me. Guide me. Allow me to step into the role that You have designed for me."

Chapter 5

MY ASSIGNMENT

...Call upon me in the day of trouble; I will deliver
you, and you will honor me.

—Psalm 50:15

JENNY VAN NORDEN, AFFECTIONATELY known as "Oma,"
called one evening with words I was dreading. My mentor,
friend, and second father in the Lord, John Van Norden, had
gone home to be with Jesus. Of course, we were in one of those
busy times at the funeral home, and that meant meeting the
needs of multiple families, handling the many details, bringing
sincere care to the situation, and also juggling the activity at
home all at the same time. In other words, I was frazzled, and,
like John Hobbs said at the 1987 men's conference I mentioned

earlier, "I was *peopled*." When people need us from every direction, we often try to give and give, until we get to the point that
we just do not want to see another person, and *Wham!* something happens that slams us up against the wall of working in
our own strength. I hit that wall when the call came from St.
Simons Island. My first thought was, *Oh Lord, You've got to help
me! How can I possibly bring anything of value to the table in my
current state of mind?*

Just shortly before, I had discovered a new way of looking at
story, and it was apparent that my story was still being developed.
John Eldredge had spoken to the core of my being, and God was
calling me to find my place in His story. I remembered one of John's
most popular books, and I wondered if I had been asleep. I was
convinced that God had a word hidden for me in the pages of *Wild
at Heart*, and I knew that I had to go back and revisit that book.

Sometimes it's possible to hear and not really hear, and it's also
possible to see and not really see. That's what happened with me
during my first reading of *Wild at Heart*. As I opened the pages
for the second time, in the context of John Van Norden's passing,
God used the book to open a window in my heart that had been
sealed for a long time. God's timing is amazing, and I was about
midway in my second read when I received the call from Oma.

John, Jenny, and I had very carefully and intentionally planned
every detail of his funeral ahead of time. They wanted me to be
involved with directing the funeral, leading worship, singing his
favorite hymn, and sharing one of my favorite "Opa" stories to
lead off the eulogy time. April and the girls were covered up with

school and could not adjust their schedules to travel with me to St. Simons, so I made arrangements to fly south. I knew that I desperately needed an intimate time with God on the trip.

Invariably when I travel, I visit with other travelers and don't take personal quiet time. This time, I needed to be alone with God. I begged Him to please give me privacy on the trip. I prayed that I could sit alone to Atlanta, and right up to the very last person, the seat beside me was still vacant. I was amazed, but as I looked up, I noticed one last man making his way down the aisle, and the only seat I could see open was 14B. Of course, that was the one I wanted to stay empty. My heart sank when he took his seat, but, as he settled in, I said, "Okay God, I trust you," I welcomed him with my typical greeting. He had that deer-in-the-headlights look and said, in Spanish, "*Hola.*" I just laughed inside, knowing that probably the only non-English speaking person on the plane was sitting beside me. I thanked Jesus and opened my book, getting lost in words that were leading me to a deep hidden place in my heart.

The layover in Atlanta was brief, and I made my way to the small jet for the flight to Brunswick, Georgia. I wondered how God would make a private place for me on such a small plane, but I had an overwhelming sense of anticipation that He was going to meet with me before the end of the flight. I made my way to my assigned seat in the very back of the jet and no one was sitting in either of the last two rows. What a setup! I opened *Wild at Heart* again and was reading the passage in which Eldredge was describing a grueling trip and his need to hear from God. This sounded like my situation. I cannot explain the stirring in my heart, but I knew the Lord was close. I sat up in my seat and read this prayer:

> "What of me, dear Lord? Are you pleased? What did you see? I am sorry that I have to ask, wishing I knew without asking. Fear, I suppose, makes me doubt. Still, I yearn to hear from you—a word, or image, a name or even just a glance from You."
>
> This is what I heard.
>
> "You are Henry V after Agincourt...the man in the arena, whose face is covered with blood and sweat and dust, who strove valiantly...a great warrior...yes, even Maximus."
>
> And then "You are my friend."*

As I read these words, I strongly felt the presence of the Holy Spirit; it was as if Jesus himself sat with me. I could almost feel His arm slide around my shoulder and hear Him say to me, "*And you are my friend; I approve of you, and I want to spend time with you, like this, every day.*" All my life I have searched for approval, and God knew that I needed to hear him speak that word of life to me. I wept uncontrollably for several minutes, feeling freedom and hope like never before. Strangely, I found myself answering Him with, "But I don't have time." He then said, "*If you will spend private time with me, I will multiply your time, and you will know that I am with you.*"

---

* John Eldredge, *Wild at Heart: Discovering the Secret of a Man's Soul,* (Nashville: Thomas Nelson, 2001) p. 135.

Finally, I felt God saying that I should focus on ministry to the men around me. It seemed that He was saying, *"Follow John Van Norden's lead and* give *to everyone in your life…forget about Ted."*

My time with the Van Norden family was such a blessing, and the funeral was indeed a release and a celebration of Opa's home-going. The saints rejoiced at home and in heaven. There was very little private time with Oma, but, before my departure, Jenny spoke an amazing blessing over me. It came as no surprise that it confirmed the words of Colossians 3:2, words the Lord had spoken to me on my journey to the island: "Set your mind on things above, not on earthly things."

The story didn't end there! Some years later, our family was visiting Oma and sharing precious memories. We worshiped, prayed, and cried together. As we shared, I was reminded of her boldness and praise. It took me back and opened the window to one of the most sincere and genuine acts of worship I've ever witnessed.

It was as if time stood still while the world tried to grasp and assimilate the implications of the terrorist attacks that September 11th, 2001. That same day, in a small hospital room, the surgeon had his eyes buried in his notes, carefully considering how he would communicate Opa's prognosis to his family. As he raised his head from the medical charts, he witnessed a profound display of hope. Eight of John's closest friends were on their knees, surrounding his bed and praying for the Kingdom to come and for God's will to be done on earth as it is in heaven. Oma danced before the Lord, praying for healing and life.

God answered that night's prayers in a way that gave the Van Nordens three more years to enjoy together, and they never gave up on the message of the Kingdom and the goodness of God. Some thirty years earlier, they discovered life and the fullness of the gospel, and this couple lived every moment with reckless abandon, knowing Jesus and making Him known!

In God's timing, those three blessed years of reprieve came to a close, and an EMS crew was called to their home in response to Opa's condition. Again, Oma danced, trusting Jesus. They made the trip to the hospital, and, once again, after Jesus came to his room and took Opa home, Oma danced...

As previously noted, John, Jenny, and I pre-planned every detail of the funeral. Every detail, that is, except for one special, spontaneous act of praise.

We all worshiped with confidence during the funeral and celebrated Opa's life with scriptures, songs, and stories. And then, for me, came the sweetest moment of all: Oma danced! Later, I asked her how she danced at the funeral. Oma replied with a glow, "How could I not? We lived every breath with the anticipation of seeing Jesus, and my Bearkins is now with our Savior!"

In the intimacy of her home, we witnessed the power of the Kingdom and her personal proclamation of healing and hope. In that precious moment, she was transferring her blessing to us, and it affirmed my mission to pass the same gift on to you!

After the funeral and over the next year, my relationship with Jesus became more real and intimate than I had ever dreamed possible. God more than kept His promise. He multiplied my time and met me in the secret place day after day. My well expanded and the river seemed to be flowing like a broken dam with an eternal supply. I seemed to be accomplishing more in every aspect of life including family, work, relationships, Bible study, and especially my pursuit of the Kingdom of heaven. During one of those quiet times, the Lord said, "*You finally understand that verse you've quoted hundreds of times.*" That verse is Matthew 6:33: "But seek first his kingdom and his righteousness, and all these things will be given to you as well." The Kingdom of heaven is not just a place for us to live after death; it's the reality of heaven that Jesus intended for us to live in between here and there. It is the truth that sets us free!

I was discovering the secret of contentment that the Word speaks about in Philippians 4:11. Almost one year after the funeral, Pastor Bill Johnson was scheduled to be at a conference in Pennsylvania, and three of us decided to go. Once again, I felt like I needed God to clarify business or ministry, and, very simply, from a word given by Lance Walnau, I heard God say, "*Do both.*" God spoke to each of us in a very powerful way, and He affirmed that we all had purpose and destiny right in the small town of Reidsville, North Carolina.

It was clear that God had not released me from funeral service, so I knew that I had to dig in to discover God's plan for me in my work as a funeral director. The more I learned about the Kingdom of God and the reality of heaven in my personal walk, the more I began to realize how critical it is for this Kingdom reality to be used in the equation for life after loss and disappointment.

It seemed that every sermon I was hearing and everything I was reading was leading me to consider how to bring *life* to the funeral home. God was showing me that He has a message of hope and life for the families who are facing the most difficult times and the very darkest days.

To my surprise, God has been using the years of funeral service to get me to a place of confidence in Him and a level of credibility in the business that would allow me to put the two together. He was calling me to communicate His solution to death, loss, and disappointment. "Okay," I said, "Lord, where do I start? It's me, Ted, from Reidsville." He said, "*You are my son. I knew you before you were born, and I want you to write.*" Writing works for me about as well as a screen door works in a submarine. In order for me to write a book, a miracle of God would be necessary.

I verbalized my assignment to the other men in my Tuesday morning Bible study, and it was as if God had already told them. There was no hesitation, only encouragement and questions about my plans. I knew then that God was in it. God was speaking to me day and night with ideas. I would fall asleep thinking about the Kingdom. I would dream about the stories God wanted me to share, and I would wake up with a sense of urgency to do something a.s.a.p.

I pressed in to hear the heart of God, needing clarity for the focus of my book. I knew I needed to somehow reveal the Kingdom's impact on loss, and yet it could not sound like a funeral book. It had to be *full* of life. Day and night, I prayed diligently for about three weeks, and one night my middle daughter, Amelia, and I decided to watch the movie *The Guardian*. After reading John Eldredge, I now always look for the gospel in movies and ask God to speak His truth in the story. Anyone who has seen the movie will understand what I mean when I say the story reveals the servant heart of the rescue swimmers. Their purpose is to save lives. As the movie came to a close, the tragedy of the story unfolded, and we were sitting there stunned in disbelief. In the stillness of a huge setting sun, the silhouette of a helicopter passed by, and the caption below read, "So others may live"; I was overcome with God's "still small voice," and I knew in that moment the direction and concept for this book.

The purpose of Jesus and His Kingdom is to give us life! Satan will use whatever he can to take life from us, including tragedy, disappointment, sickness, and, ultimately, the death of our loved ones. The contrast is clearly defined in John 10:10: "The thief comes only to steal, kill, and destroy; I have come that they may have life and have it to the full."

God has used the circumstances of my life story to bring me to this place. Now God wants me to share some of these biblical lessons of life and hope about his Kingdom that can help set us increasingly free from the cruel world of loss and disappointment. As we unfold this message together, four stories about families that have endured tragedy and loss are offered as examples of God's work in the darkest of circumstances. The power of their testimonies can help us discover and be reminded of the practical, radical, supernatural, redemptive hand of God.

Then I heard a loud voice in heaven say: "Now have come the salvation and the power and the kingdom of our God, and the authority of his Christ. For the accuser of our brothers, who accuses them before our God day and night, has been hurled down. They overcame him by the blood of the Lamb and by the word of their testimony; they did not love their lives so much as to shrink from death."

—Revelation 12:10-11

IN THE KINGDOM OF GOD WE FIND OUR HOPE FOR HEALING

I WANT THERE TO BE no doubt about my passion and purpose. Most people say that remembering the loss of a loved one reminds them of their darkest days. As I witness this over and over, it fuels the burning desire in me to release light and life to the equation. We can walk out of darkness into the marvelous light. We can be open to change in the way we think and discover this Kingdom that Jesus has established for us to live in and to experience every day! The enemy uses loss and disappointment to distract us from the Kingdom of life that is within reach. He wants to keep us in the dark!

Four families have entrusted me with the histories of their darkest days, believing that their circumstances will release healing, hope, and a future for others. The example of Jesus proved that the power of the testimony is far superior to clever words, creative writing, or conjured stories. I pray the Holy Spirit uses each story here to encourage hearts and illuminate the biblical truths in this book.

These chapters are not intended to elevate the families and their stories, but to encourage us to look beyond our situations to find hope. I pray we will all realize greater depth of understanding and spiritual power through the healing and abundant life Jesus brings.

Chapter 6

THE KINGDOM

Repent, for the Kingdom of heaven is near.
—Matthew 4:17b

WHY WOULD JESUS START His earthly ministry with this statement? Why, up to this point, have I made so many references to the "Kingdom of heaven" or the "Kingdom of God"?

Jesus wanted to make clear, from the very beginning of His ministry, the relevance of the Kingdom message. As a matter of fact, I'm convinced that He started here because understanding the difference between the earthly kingdom we live in and the Kingdom of heaven is, no doubt, paramount to the entire purpose and plan of God. In the original Greek, Jesus was saying, "The Kingdom of heaven is here, in other words, it has *arrived*." He was actually establishing the fact that He was bringing the reality of heaven to earth for our benefit.

The word *repent* was critical because *repent* doesn't just mean to be sorry for what we've done but to experience a genuine change of mind. In other words, we must change the way we think. In order to receive this Kingdom that Jesus brought to earth, we must think differently from what we've been taught. We've been conditioned to think by the visual, by the here and now. The reality of earth tends to be our benchmark for our expectations of who God is and what He can do. Beyond that, we tend to look toward heaven and lose sight of the fact that the Kingdom that Jesus taught throughout the New Testament establishes the fullness of our relationship with Jesus here on earth, *now*.

At some point and one way or another, each of us has either already walked through loss and disappointment or we will. This is not a case of calling out bad things; this is just the reality of life experience. We live in a fallen world, and satan's intention is to take death, broken marriages, lost jobs, or anything else that is important in life and magnify those things so that he can keep us in a place of darkness. He knows that as long as our attention remains on the loss, we remain helpless and hopeless. Almost daily I see people trying to grasp for solutions to the hurt they feel from the loss of loved ones. We want relief and hope, and it is critical that we know early on that Paul clearly explains, "For the kingdom of God is not a matter of eating and drinking, but of righteousness, peace and joy in the Holy Spirit" (Rom. 14:17). Jesus brings life, and we will dig deeper into righteousness, peace, and joy a little later.

I'm not going to try to convince anyone that loss and disappointment won't come. I'm not going to try and determine why it comes to some and not to others or especially why the circumstances of some are more dramatic or violent. What I am going to do is to communicate that God has life and a plan for us and that He sent his Son to reestablish our place of authority here on earth. That place is found in His Kingdom. This is *not* about church busyness or being religious. It is all about a relationship with the King and who we are because of it. It's about discovering the life He brings into every situation.

FAITH

We can look beyond our normal perspective to consider our circumstances through the eyes of faith. What is faith? "Now faith is being sure of what we hope for and certain of what we do not see" (Heb. 11:1). Verse three of the same chapter explains that God as creator made the visible world that we see out of the invisible. Creation is the perfect example of faith. God set the standard and faith is a big deal. Hebrews 11:6 says: "And without faith it is impossible to please God, because anyone who comes to him must believe that he exists and that he rewards those who earnestly seek him." I like Pastor Bill Johnson's description of this. He says that "Faith is anchored in the unseen (the invisible) and unbelief is anchored in the seen (the visible). The seen world includes everything that is natural and physical (the reality of earth), while the unseen implies everything that is supernatural

(the reality of heaven)."* The perspective we need is described in 2 Corinthians 4:18: "So we fix our eyes not on what is seen, but on what is unseen. For what is seen is temporary but what is unseen is eternal." We must pursue the superior reality and those things that are eternal.

Think of this; unbelief is equated to fear. Fear is established in that place where we come into agreement with satan's threats. If we agree with his lies, it leads to deception and ultimately ends up as unbelief. If satan can keep us in a place of fear, then he can use unbelief to keep us from the awareness that God *can* invade our circumstances. Unfortunately, loss and disappointment tend to lead us to the here and now. Satan understands our weaknesses and our dependence on relationship. Considering the loss of a loved one, he takes that relationship and distorts it to the point that we get caught up in the mire of the natural and earthly. Thus, satan wants to make it almost impossible for us to refocus on God or His word.

One of the best biblical stories of "small faith lessons learned" is in Mark 4: 35-41. The disciples and Jesus are heading across the water in their boat, and the storm is referred to as a "furious squall." The disciples are terrified and Jesus is sleeping. As soon as the disciples wake Jesus, He calms the storm. Then in verse 41, the gentle rebuke is given in that very teachable moment: "He said to His disciples, 'Why are you so afraid? Do you still have no faith?'" He was basically saying, fearfulness is the same as

---

* Bill Johnson, "The Nature of Faith," (sermon, Redding, CA: Bethel Church).

faithlessness. God wants us to trust Him. Faith, therefore, must be part of the equation. Think back to what I said earlier: in order for us to embrace faith, we must repent and change the way we think. Like Dr. Myles Munroe says, "If a man's thinking doesn't change, the man doesn't change."*

THE KINGDOM OF GOD

Jesus said, "And this gospel of the kingdom will be preached in the whole world as a testimony to all nations, and then the end will come" (Matt. 24:14). Why would Jesus say the "gospel" of the Kingdom? It's the "good news" of the Kingdom that must be proclaimed. It amazes me to see that, after the resurrection of Jesus, the Bible clearly communicates that, "He appeared to them over a period of forty days and spoke about the kingdom of God" (Acts 1:3b). It's apparent that the message of the Kingdom was significant. He also said "I must preach the good news of the kingdom of God to the other towns also, because that is why I was sent" (Luke 4:43). At one point, Jesus sent out the twelve disciples in order for them to get a glimpse of this message. He told them, "As you go, preach this message: 'The kingdom of heaven is near.' Heal the sick, raise the dead, cleanse those who have leprosy, drive out demons. Freely you have received, freely give" (Matt. 10:7-8). It's obvious that this Kingdom has something to do with power.

---

* Dr. Myles Munroe, "The Kingdom Series: Contrasting Kingdoms" (sermon, Nassau, Bahamas: The Diplomat Center).

Paul explains it later when he says, "For the kingdom of God is not a matter of talk, but of power" (1 Cor. 4:20).

Genesis 1:26-31 explains God's original purpose and plan for us. In Dr. Myles Munroe's third sermon of his amazing series on the Kingdom, he gives a masterful explanation of the Kingdom "Dominion Mandate." First, God wanted to establish His heavenly Kingdom on earth through mankind. God made us like Himself so that we could have dominion over the earth. He intended for us to rule over everything. Because He made us with that in mind, He made sure that we had everything we needed to fulfill the task. For example, he made birds to fly, so he gave them the ability to fly. And, likewise, verse 26 says, "Let us make man in our image, in our likeness, and let them rule...." We were created to rule under God's authority. God made us intentionally, just the way we are, for His purpose. Before we were conceived, God had an idea for His Kingdom purpose, and that idea finds its fulfillment in each of us as we respond to His grace and His Kingdom call! Deep inside of every heart, God has a divine plan waiting to be revealed and followed step by step. Regardless of how we feel right now or at any given moment, the truth is this: God loves us! We are His children, and He loves us in His eternal and omnipresent ways! Do we really understand this? God *loves* us! What I'm really trying to say is, GOD LOVES US!!!

SONSHIP

He wanted His Kingdom to be shared with His family. Unlike an earthly kingdom, God wanted to establish a Kingdom of sons, not servants. Jesus explained this principle using the story of the lost son. In Luke 15:11-31, Jesus explained the young son who had squandered his inheritance and found himself eating with the pigs, and he realized that even the servants back home had it better than he. So he decided that he would return home and ask forgiveness and hope to be restored, at least as a servant. But when he returned, his father was waiting, and with open arms of restoration, the father restored him as *son,* not as a servant. "But the father said to his servants, 'Quick! Bring the best robe and put it on him. Put a ring on his finger and sandals on his feet. Bring the fattened calf and kill it. Let's have a feast and celebrate. For this son of mine was dead and is alive again; he was lost and is found.' So they began to celebrate" (Luke 15:22-24). This is a picture of God waiting to restore us as son or daughter. He wants to lavish us with the fullness of His Kingdom.

I'm convinced that this is where many believers lose sight of their birthright. God creates everyone born on this earth in His image, for His purpose. Because of Adam's sin, we lost our rights and authority here on earth. Actually, satan took the keys of authority. Jesus came to restore the original plan of God, and in the great commission, He made it clear that He had, "Then Jesus came to them and said, 'All authority in heaven and on earth has been given to me'" (Matt. 28:18). Earlier Jesus proclaimed to the disciples, "I will give you the keys of the kingdom of heaven:

whatever you bind on earth will be bound in heaven, and what-ever you loose on earth will be loosed in heaven" (Matt. 16:19). He later finished the prophetic word by proclaiming, "I am the Living One; I was dead, and behold I am alive for ever and ever! And I hold the keys of death and Hades" (Rev. 1:18).

When we return to the Father and ask God's forgiveness for our sins, we *are* His sons and daughters. That means that we get *all* that comes with being in the family. Jesus is our brother, and all that is His, is ours. Jesus said, "Believe me when I say that I am in the Father and the Father is in me; or at least believe on the evidence of the miracles themselves. I tell you the truth, anyone who has faith in me will do what I have been doing. He will do even greater things than these, because I am going to the Father" (John 14:11-12).

We have no need to sell ourselves short. This is where faith comes alive. Jesus said, "Therefore I tell you, whatever you ask for in prayer, believe that you have received it, and it will be yours" (Mark 11:24). We can believe that we have received our inheri-tance and live in it.

God did not go through all that I mentioned above just for us to go to heaven. Of course, heaven is going to be awesome, but He carefully designed this redemption plan so that we can *live* in victory—today. We don't have to wait to go to heaven; the Kingdom of heaven is at hand.

Remember, when God restores us as we accept Jesus as Lord, we have been given authority to rule. Psalm 115:16 verifies this view: "The highest heavens belong to the LORD, but the earth he has given to man." So, in other words, we are called to rule over the earth. Stated another way, our domain is earth and we are called to be the ruler or king of that domain. We become the Kingdom of God on earth. The Kingdom is not the earth, but it is how we carry out our dominion on the planet. Actually, the Word says, "...the kingdom of God is within you" (Luke 17:21b). It's almost like saying that the reality of heaven comes alive in us when by faith we embrace our divine purposes as designed by God. Then, and only then, can the Kingdom of heaven be released through us on earth. When we realize our purposes, life explodes in hope and meaning.

It's interesting that Jesus taught us to pray, "your Kingdom come, your will be done on earth as it is in heaven" (Matt. 6:10). He knew that the reality of heaven *is* superior to the reality of earth, and He communicated from the very beginning that He brought the solution to earth with His Kingdom. Jesus spent His entire ministry teaching the disciples about the Kingdom of God. Ironically, just a few verses later, Jesus says, "But seek first his kingdom and his righteousness, and all these things will be given to you as well" (Matt. 6:33). What He was actually saying is that His Kingdom comes fully equipped to meet every need.

We must change the way we think! If we maintain merely a servant's attitude, we will remain in a place of defeat. We are sons and daughters of God, children of the *King*! God has designed this kingdom so that we can step out of that place of hopelessness. Instead of being ruled, we can stand in the face of that demon of despair and proclaim, "Your assignment is cancelled, and I'm stepping into my rightful place as son or daughter of the King." We can claim our Kingdom rights and enjoy its benefits.

The next chapter shares how the Johnson family stumbled into tragedy with their son, and then how the message of the Kingdom of God released life and hope at home and throughout their community.

CHAPTER 7

A STORY OF TRAGEDY, HOPE, AND THE KINGDOM OF HEAVEN

EDGAR WILLIAM "WILL" JOHNSON
May 7, 1983 ~ September 8, 2000

&

JAMES BAILEY JOHNSON
October 2, 1985 ~ May 7, 1986

*Edgar William "Will" Johnson With the
Blessing of the Johnson family*

O N LABOR DAY WEEKEND, 2000, late Friday night, Dr. Larry Price opened the door to the lake cottage and found a room full of children wild with excitement. "You should have seen the play! Will took an end around sweep ninety-four yards for a touchdown!" Edgar William "Will" Johnson had returned to his dad's old high school to hopefully reestablish the football legacy and dominance of Harrell's Christian Academy. This was the resurgence of the hope of glory and the taste of victory known by the Academy's past ten state championships.

The Johnsons have been a longtime Harrell's family, supporting the school over the years. A few years earlier, Cowan, the Johnsons' oldest son, had made the decision to return to the local public high school, Wallace-Rose Hill. The Johnsons agreed that the change was right both academically and athletically. Following his brother's lead, Will had also chosen to go to Wallace-Rose

Hill. In his dad's words, "Will was *the man* his freshman season," and the coach moved him up to varsity his sophomore year. Even though Will had great potential, his size and inexperience left him standing on the sideline, and the whole Johnson family felt frustrated with the lack of playing time. Soon after the school year, Will felt the tug to return to Harrell's Christian Academy. The football program was in a rebuilding mode, and he was confident he could make an impact. He was a young man with vision and had the desire to succeed academically, athletically, personally, and spiritually. He felt his return to the Christian school environment would facilitate his growth in every way. The family embraced his decision and supported him completely.

Being a longtime football family, the Johnsons stepped up and immediately rejoined the booster support team. Will's parents, Bob and Luanne, had always been supportive of his athletic endeavors, like they were with his older brother, Cowan, and his younger brother, Nash Julian. His little sister, Carole Luanne, was his number one cheerleader. During our meeting, Bob actually confessed to me that football had almost become his "god." This team had the chance to win, so he and a couple of the other dads met with the coach and pressed him to get serious about turning this football program around. That meant hard work and practice on Labor Day, for cryin' out loud!

For the Crusaders' third game, the Johnsons invited the football team to their home for a pre-game meal. By keeping the team together before the game, they all agreed the boys would be more focused on Friday night business and winning the football game.

The food was an energy meal, laden with pasta and all of the fixin's.

Bob shared some old Harrell's football stories, and Luanne gave the team a motivational word of encouragement and hope for the game. She told them, "Win as a team, and lose as a team; no position is more important than another. There are no heroes here; we are one. We are one in Christ, and since He's the One who gives us the ability to play, let's give Him the glory for tonight's game." Will hugged his mom and dad before hopping on the activity bus and heading off to the game. Cowan also made it home from college in time to see Will and the team off.

Excitement was in the air; after the shot of the cannon and the ringing of Luanne's cowbell, the September 8 football game had begun! Harrell's was making its way down the field for a score and fumbled. Wake Christian recovered and started a drive of its own. It was deep in the first quarter, fourth and about a foot to go for the first down. Wake decided to go for it! Playing "safety," Will read the play and from the wide side of the field came across and stopped the first down attempt.

"It was a good tackle, a good play, a good collision. Nothing out of the ordinary," said Coach Bron Thompson.[*] The tailback saw Will and lowered his head hoping to gain the necessary yardage and sailed helmet first into #34.

The team rallied around Will with high fives, and the crowd was ecstatic: Harrell's ball, first and ten. Unfortunately, Will knew

---

[*] Kyle Foster, "A Football School Mourns," *Fayetteville Observer*, September 10, 2000.

that something was wrong. He took about five steps toward the sideline and said to the coach, "Coach, you've got to take me out!" The coach looked to the sideline to find a replacement and turned back to the confusion of seeing Will, face down, lifeless on the field. Silence fell on the stadium as tragedy raced into the hearts of all who witnessed Will drop. Of course, Bob was working the sidelines and was able to make his way to his son's side almost immediately. Will actually stopped breathing on the field, but Dr. Quinn, who was attending the game, rode in the ambulance, working on him all the way to the hospital. Bob and Luanne rode in the front seat of the ambulance.

In her desperation, Luanne had always expected Bob to be able to fix whatever had come their way, and she cried out, "Bob, you've got to fix this!" His reply was simply, "Just pray!" She knew at that moment that the situation was really bad, and her only refuge was God, because Bob couldn't fix it.

Allow me to interject that I asked a difficult question before we could move forward with the story. I asked them to describe where they were spiritually at this point of their lives, and, without hesitation, they said, "We were religious." Bob said he felt as though church was just like any other club, and it was something he had "to do." They were busy helping out with church activities and went to church when they could but did not understand what it meant to have a personal relationship with Jesus.

Ironically, they both agreed that something changed in the ambulance. In describing the ride to the hospital, Bob said that he felt the presence of God like never before, and he knew that the

Holy Spirit, "the Comforter", had arrived to carry them through this darkness. In his words, it was just that: darkness. "I knew that God would get us through this, but I didn't know how. I was completely ignorant to the Word, which confirms that I was living in darkness. I needed to get in the light to find the hope and the answers that would bring us life."

During the many interviews, Bob would always say, "God is going to get us through this, but I don't really know how, but He will." It was interesting that people were almost offended at the Johnsons' unfailing trust in God and the confidence in His eventual healing and breakthrough. With delight, Bob looked at me and said, "What I would have liked to have been able to say is, see me seven years from now." In that moment, hope and life filled the room.

Going back to the turmoil at the stadium, both teams' players and fans converged onto the field, joining in prayer and watching in disbelief as the Johnsons rode away together in the ambulance. The game was called off, and many people from both teams made their way to the hospital to support the family.

There were many unsuccessful attempts to revive Will, but he was pronounced dead later that night at a local medical facility. As the tragic news spread through the area, around the state, and ultimately on the sports AP national news, everyone wondered how the Johnson family would handle this devastating turn of events. How could this be happening again to the same family?

Fifteen years prior to this September tragedy, the Johnsons were planning the arrival of their third baby and soon celebrated the birth of James Bailey Johnson. The family was excited with the arrival of the new addition to the family but quickly discovered that Bailey had respiratory problems. He also had, they thought, a slight heart murmur and, over the coming months, a prolonged jaundice. Their doctor was concerned over the lengthy jaundice and suggested that the Johnsons go to a specialist in Chapel Hill. While they were there, the doctor felt they should see a pediatric cardiologist. The results proved to be a life-changing piece of news. Bailey was diagnosed with a Vesicular Stomatitis Virus (VSV) heart defect, a large hole between the left and right ventricles of the heart. From that time, the family circumstances became more and more difficult with Bailey in and out of the hospital. As his breathing continued to become more compromised, the specialist suggested the need for open-heart surgery (a surgery that was supposed to be 98 percent successful.) The Johnsons felt secure with the positive probability of success and decided to move forward with the surgery. In very short order and within 24 hours of the surgery, it was apparent that Bailey would fall in that 2 percent category. How could this be? A family with vision, hope, dreams, and now the death of their son, May 7th, 1986, Will's third birthday. How would they start over, and where was God?

Bailey's death was very painful for the Johnsons, and Luanne fell deeply into the mire of self-pity and grief. Bitterness and darkness tried desperately to destroy her. Her anger with God grew as she tried to understand why He would give them a child, less than perfect. Why them and not someone else? This was a family of faith, but their whole foundation seemed shaky, at best.

Over the next few months, the depression increased, but one morning, Luanne seemed to hear the Holy Spirit whispering, *"Wake up. Satan is trying to steal you and your family. He is taking your weakness and winding his purpose into your lives."* She knew that she was at a crossroad. She could trust God's will or satan's lies. Luanne and Bob chose to trust God.

Slowly, but surely, healing came. The Johnsons found themselves giving to others in their time of need. Luanne especially discovered that, through her own adversity, God was developing an encouragement ministry through her as she so readily reached out to others who were hurting. Once again, her family seemed secure, as the six Johnsons entered the new millennium...

Even though this couple survived the devastating loss and death of Bailey, in their reflection back to that painful season, Bob admitted that he just moved forward with work, family, and football. He was a believer, but in his words, "I was very much in the world. I would have gone to heaven, but I was ignorant. I was living in darkness and just did not know the difference."

Baileys' death and all the pain experienced unexpectedly laid the foundation for this family to forge through the tragic events of September 8, 2000.

Seventeen year-old Daniel Price, one of Will's closest friends, felt helpless as he and his friends waited at the hospital for some word of encouragement. He called his mother, Cynthia, and said, "Mom, he's dead!" Being one of Luanne's closest friends, Cynthia knew that this would be one of the most difficult crossroads imaginable. Close to one hundred friends and family stood devastated as the news of Will's death spread from one to the other. The Harrell's, Rose Hill, and Wallace communities would never be the same.

Bob's mind raced back to Bailey's death, reminding him of the pain before, and all he could think was, *This can't be happening again.* Bob says, "All I could think about were the things that we went through with Bailey, which was horrible." As Luanne affirmed those early horrible moments, in spite of the devastation, she described how healing started almost immediately. A sister who had been estranged from the family over the recent years made her way to the hospital and has, since that time, reestablished a relationship with the family and with the Lord; within hours of Will's death, the redemptive hand of God was at work.

Cowan, Will's older brother, was devastated. When the family arrived at Luanne's mother's home, he was confused and broken. He went out on the terrace alone and begged God to give him something to hope for. He asked God to please give him a sign that Will was there with Him, and as he looked into the heavens, almost instantly, a shooting star crossed the skies in full view. Often after that first time, shooting stars seemed to cross the sky at the most amazing times and became a symbol of hope. When we have eyes to see and ears to hear, the supernatural voice of God often speaks through nature.

Luanne felt compelled to speak at the funeral. Even in the midst of her overwhelming pain, she felt the salvation message had to be proclaimed to the hundreds attending the service. She knew that somehow there had to be hope for the multitudes of young people at the funeral. There was an overflow crowd as the Johnsons endured the burial of yet another son.

This family ran to the cross and became focused on their pursuit of Jesus. Regardless of how things looked, they would trust God. Three months after Will's death, the Lord opened a door for the Johnsons to establish a praise and worship, encouragement ministry called, "The Living Will Ministry." The family and some very close friends worked together sharing their testimony and the message of salvation and hope. Some weeks, they performed and spoke in as many as three different cities. Through their obedience and service, God has worked in the lives of hundreds of people in churches all over the east coast.

As the family worked, prayed, and sought God, the Holy Spirit was at work teaching and guiding them in the most miraculous ways. Luanne went back to school to study the Bible, and Bob joined an early morning men's Bible study. Because we perish for the lack of knowledge, they both decided that they would chase the light (knowledge) that would destroy the darkness (lack of knowledge). Steve Larue introduced Bob to the teachings of Dr. Myles Monroe, and the gospel of the Kingdom came to life in their hearts. The river of living water was released. I remember my friend, Dr. Larry Price, telling me that Bob said, "I've been in church all my life, and I've never heard this good news before. There's power and life, and it's right within reach."

When Nash graduated from high school, the dynamics of the Living Will Ministry changed. Bob and Luanne were experiencing what's often called "the renewing of the mind," and Bob wanted everyone to hear this message. The efforts of the ministry shifted, and they started a new ministry outreach called "Crossroads," an interdenominational meeting designed to proclaim the gospel of the Kingdom. Bob invited Steve Larue to be the teacher, and the Sunday morning meetings gained momentum each week.

Over the course of the next several months, the Johnsons also invited Steve into their home for deeper Bible study and fellowship. After a frightening incident with their daughter, the Lord spoke to Steve revealing the fact that there seemed to be a curse on the family. He asked about early death in their history, and as Bob and Luanne looked back, they realized that early death had indeed invaded both sides of their families for generations. Bob understood that satan could only have the authority that we give him, and with Steve's help, the Johnsons agreed with their God-given inheritance in the Kingdom and broke that generational curse.

Since that time, the fresh wind of the Spirit seems to be blowing wherever the Johnsons go. A group of the faithful ones attending the Crossroads meetings felt the need to take the Kingdom message to the next level and began a new fellowship called "Kingdom Builders." This group meets with anticipation, hope, and life. With the Johnsons continuing the Crossroads ministry, excitement and revival are chasing throughout the whole community. As I shared a meal with them at a local restaurant one evening, everyone who passed by stopped to talk about Jesus. It was *so* refreshing!

Two young men offered their testimonies, and I share their perspective here, briefly. First, Matt Buckner joined us and lit up the room with his enthusiasm. He talked about his friendship with Will and the havoc he experienced after the death. Matt felt completely broken and lost. He chased everything the world had to offer. He said, "When Will died, I was in the world. I was delving into drugs big time, and it seemed to be the only solution. I went to church, but I did not have a relationship with Jesus." It was obvious that Matt walked through a time of depression and self-destruction. He said, "A man would rather spend a day in the field with his worst enemy, than one night alone in a closet with himself."

Then he told me this story:

> The last time I went to church was about one-and-a-half years ago. I had been out of the church for about three years and not one person came up to me and said, 'I love you.' Not one person said, 'I've missed you.' I had my suit on, and it was closing in on me. As soon as the preacher prayed, I left. Walking home, I cried out to God and said, 'If this is all you've got, I don't want it any more.' I even challenged God. 'I'll give you two weeks or I'm leaving this place.'

The next week, Matt walked into the Crossroads meeting and heard the life message of the Kingdom. He's never been the same.

Second, the Johnsons' nephew, Curtis Carr, who was also on the team with his older cousin Will, joined us that morning. He mentioned how excited he was to have had the opportunity to play with Will. After the accident, Curtis mainly remembered the confusion and turmoil of the game. Will's death shook his world. Football worked for Curtis, and he actually played his freshman year at Furman University. He joined a fraternity, partied hard, and just gave in to everything the world offered. He finally realized that he was on a slow train to nowhere, and he asked God for help. The summer after his sophomore year, he entered the housing lottery, and, of course, he landed in a room with three Christian roommates.

One of the roommates, Win Bauman, was also in a desperate place with his life. Curtis said, "I had no other options! I was looking for something that could save my life from the destructive train I was on, and I decided to go back to church and give God another chance. At the same time, Win was sick of religion, and he knew that there had to be more." They had heard positive things about Redemption World Outreach Center and decided to go for it.

When they visited Redemption, the Kingdom message and the Presence of God was almost overwhelming. Curtis said, "I didn't expect that I would discover more than I had ever heard before about the gospel. The Kingdom message was an authentic, radical expression of the God of the universe, and by learning that the Holy Spirit could speak to me, I began to hear His voice! There was power within reach and this gospel was for *real*." He discovered life and had an authentic encounter with the King. He's never been the same…

Here is one final story about Nash, the Johnsons' youngest son. In the midst of this two-day visit to Rose Hill, it was apparent that Nash was still hurting and angry. He had no interest in talking to me about his brother. I felt in my heart that God had something in the near future for this talented young man.

Just three weeks later, Curtis was scheduled to share his testimony, and Luanne asked Nash to go. Nash had been writing a song about Curtis (he thought), and was irritated to stop his progress on the song. Actually, he was reluctant to go to the meeting at all. Nash had the feeling that something was going to happen, and he wasn't sure that he was ready to let God invade his world. Bob felt the Holy Spirit urging him to just stay home and pray. Nash finally agreed, and when he arrived, he felt the presence of God like never before.

As Curtis was sharing, Nash was feeling hot and sweaty. He thought that it might be the Holy Spirit, and then, Frances, a close friend, came and said that God had called her to fast and pray for three days. It was obvious when she saw Nash. She had words of life for Nash, and her prophetic message broke through the hurt lodged deep in his soul. He knew in a moment that the maker of the universe loved him and that God had plans and a purpose for his future. These are the words of the song Nash was writing, "Changes":

> Well, I was out on the street, Watching people's feet,
> Wondering what has come their way,
> God bless us all, maybe we don't know
> What God does for us every day,

With these changes in me, Now, I will be,
Walking on the Streets of Gold
I was looking down, my back on the ground
Asking God to set me free,
Well, I've seen good, and I've seen bad,
And I've seen times I wish I never had,
With these changes in me, Now, I will be,
Walking on the Streets of Gold
Now I'm looking up, with a full cup,
That God has poured for me,
I see His face, I feel His grace
For I know the changes made in me
With these changes in me, Now, I will be,
Walking on the Streets of Gold,
Walking on the Streets of Gold...

—Nash Johnson

I know that I have to land this story somehow, but each time I review my visit with the Johnsons, I marvel at the amazing work of the gospel of the Kingdom and the life it nurtures. Will's parents have a prayer to share with those who face loss and reach for hope.

Luanne reviewed her marriage and the pain she and Bob have endured. Even though their faith was shaky early on, they did have a foundation built on Jesus. She said, "Even in the midst of all of the pain, suffering, and even death, God has given us *life*, not only to us but [to] so many." She also communicated the fact that, by choosing to trust God, He has blessed them with favor, and He has an assignment for them to fulfill. Statistically, 70 percent of all marriages fail after the loss of a child, not to mention the loss of two. Her prayer is that couples will pull together because their strength has grown in their hunger for the truth of the gospel. Bob has become the spiritual leader, and, like she said early in their marriage, she trusted Bob's strength in the natural, but now she trusts his strength in the supernatural.

Right on the heels of Luanne's message, Bob affirmed that even three years ago he was not in a place of strength with his understanding of the Kingdom lifestyle, but in his hunger and thirst for abundant life, he is finding strength that is indeed setting him free. His prayer and purpose is that each of us will hear this gospel of the Kingdom, embrace it, and give it to everyone who will listen. Bob wants us to understand that we do not have to live in this misery after loss and just be satisfied that we are saved and get to go to heaven one day. There is so much more. He is saying that when we get in the *light*, knowledge will bring life to us and our families. If we stay in darkness, ignorance will swallow us and satan will keep us from finding hope and purpose. Kingdom principles can affect every aspect of life, and we can taste the purpose God has for us.

The key to the Will Johnson tragedy is that this is a *life* story, and this family has discovered hope. That same hope is available to us all!

CHAPTER 8

HEALING, HOPE, AND A FUTURE

THERE IS MORE! WE need to look closely at this verse: "For the kingdom of God is not a matter of eating and drinking, but of righteousness, peace and joy in the Holy Spirit" (Rom. 14:17). There's healing, hope, and a future waiting.

I often catch myself wanting to reach deep into the sadness of the families I serve, knowing that I have to wait for the right opportunity. Sometimes it comes, but most often it does not. These are only some of the memories etched in my soul that will never be erased. I can see an amazing, brilliant, articulate, and successful man in a private moment, with the wife of over sixty years, crumble with tears as he says goodbye to his soul-mate. I envision the parents of a teenager: broken as they try to understand why their child was killed in the automobile accident. I remember weeping when I had to help a hysterical mom and her husband leave their precious baby in the cold cemetery, alone. There have been countless senior women, each one standing in tears at the head of a husband's casket, each one's prince gone, each wondering, "What am I going to do without you?" And, of course, I review my own personal memories of suicide. Every time suicide raises its ugly head at the funeral home, it's the death that satan uses to remind me of his invasion into my own past. It's his attempt to take me to a place of darkness and despair. I often feel the reality of the verse that says, "Hope deferred makes the heart sick" (Prov. 13:12a).

Instead of listening to devilish lies, I'm driven to this message of hope and life, and I'm desperate to communicate it, not only to the families I serve, but also to anyone who has ears to hear. Honestly, time and time again, I wrestle with my role as the professional "funeral director" versus the "son" with the divine purpose described previously. Needless to say, the miraculous part of the journey is the fact that, as I anchor my walk in the unseen, I grow in understanding. I become more aware of the fact that the Kingdom of heaven is within me, and it goes wherever I go. If, by faith, I believe that the reality of heaven is superior to the reality of earth, then I bring life to the equation without saying a word.

This verse calls for further consideration: "For the kingdom of God is not a matter of eating and drinking, but of righteousness, peace and joy in the Holy Spirit" (Rom. 14:17). This verse reveals that the Kingdom of God reaches beyond the tangible, physical reality of earth. When the Kingdom is established within us, renewal and redemption start with the heart. It's the fulfillment of the word given by the prophet Ezekiel, "I will give you a new heart and put a new spirit in you; I will remove from you your heart of stone and give you a heart of flesh. And I will put my Spirit in you and move you to follow my decrees and be careful to keep my laws" (Ezek. 36:26-27). With a new heart, we get different eyes to see and different ears to hear.

It's interesting to notice that the context of this passage in Romans 14 actually originated with a religious discussion on judging other believers. One of the greatest downfalls of believers comes with judgment. Paul says in the first verse of this passage, "Accept him whose faith is weak, without passing judgment on disputable matters." He makes it clear that we will all stand before God's judgment "Therefore let us stop passing judgment on one another" (v. 13). Why is this important?

The mandate is clear in Matthew 7:1-2. Jesus said, "Do not judge, or you too will be judged. For in the same way you judge others, you will be judged and with the measure you use, it will be measured to you." Yes, judging others is destructive and disruptive in every way, while the Kingdom brings life, encouragement, and hope. Jesus exemplified restoration, redemption, and life throughout His ministry. One of the most important statements at the Hopkins' house is, "We only speak life here!" The Kingdom is not just what we study, but it's who we are; it's what we give to each other, every day!

Secondly, this verse actually defines the Kingdom of God with three specific points: righteousness, peace, and joy in the Holy Spirit. *Righteousness* points to redemption and the life we find through salvation; *peace* points to freedom and the hope we find in deliverance; and *joy* points to hope and the victory we find in healing.

RIGHTEOUSNESS (SALVATION)

Throughout scripture, the righteousness of God is proclaimed. "Like your name, O God, your praise reaches to the ends of the earth; your right hand is filled with righteousness" (Ps. 48:10). "You love righteousness and hate wickedness..." (Ps. 45:7a). Not only is God righteous, but also He rules by His own righteousness. "See, a king will reign in righteousness" (Isa. 32:1a). Galatians 3:6 says Abraham "believed God, and it was accounted to him as righteousness." It's interesting that righteousness is equated with faith. When Abraham believed, the heart of God was moved. From the very beginning of the written account, God had a plan to deal with the sin problem. Our sin was one thing, but even our attempts to do good things and be good were not enough. "But we are all as an unclean thing, and all our righteousness are as filthy rags" (Isa. 64:6a, KJV). If our righteousness is detestable to God, consider our unrighteousness.

In order to put us back in right positioning with His Kingdom and to restore us as His children, God knew that He had to deal with our righteousness or the lack thereof. Isaiah 54:14, 17 says, "In righteousness you will be established; Tyranny will be far from you; you will have nothing to fear. Terror will be far removed; it will not come near you...no weapon forged against you will prevail." So let's see what Jesus did. Salvation was the first part of the Kingdom solution so that we could step into our rightful position as son or daughter. "God made him who had no sin to be sin for us, so that we might become the righteousness of God" (2 Cor. 5:21). That is the word of hope for us. By accepting the sacrifice Jesus made, we *become* the righteousness of God. That is forgiveness in the grandest sense of the word! He no longer sees sin or filthy rags; He sees His dearly loved children—completely redeemed and whole. And the blessings continue, "The fruit of righteousness will be peace; the effect of righteousness will be quietness and confidence forever" (Isa. 32:17). Wow, *freedom*! In the freedom Christ offers, God does not dwell on our past; He only sees the future, the destiny, He has in mind for us.

PEACE (DELIVERANCE)

Most of us remember the words of Isaiah in his proclamation of the coming Messiah, "For to us a child is born, to us a son is given, and the government will be on his shoulders. And he will be called Wonderful Counselor, Mighty God, Everlasting Father, *Prince of Peace*. Of the increase of his government and peace there will be no end" (Isa. 9:6-7a, emphasis added). His government (His Kingdom) will have no end and His peace will increase. The promise of Jesus rings out loud and clear: "Peace I leave with you; my peace I give you. I do not give you as the world gives. Do not let your hearts be troubled and do not be afraid" (John 14:27). This verse is so familiar and is often used as routine words at funerals, but our familiarity with it should not be an obstacle to looking more deeply into its message. Jesus, the maker of the universe, has *given* us *His* peace, the supernatural peace that calms the storm. "And he arose, and rebuked the wind, and said unto the sea, Peace, be still. And the wind ceased, and there was a great calm" (Mark 4:39, KJV). While He upholds all things by the word of His power as the Lord of creation, His peace, which goes beyond understanding, can calm the storms in our lives as well.

Even when we are awash in the wind and waves of loss and disappointment, God's peace is within reach. Paul said, "Do not be anxious about anything, but in everything, by prayer and petition, with thanksgiving, present your requests to God. And the peace of God, which transcends all understanding, will guard your hearts and your minds in Christ Jesus" (Phil. 4:6-7). This promise must be received by faith. We need not agree with satan and his lie that God doesn't care about us. We are God's children, and He loves us all—perfectly and powerfully. Paul says, "Let the peace of Christ rule in your hearts, since as members of one body you were called to peace. And be thankful" (Col. 3:15).

Lord, in the name of Jesus, I release the peace that You have released to me. Give us courage to receive Your peace, not just now, but forever! Amen.

JOY (HEALING)

Finally, God wants us to know that this peace can move us into a place of joy. "...[W]eeping may remain for a night, but rejoicing comes in the morning" (Ps. 30:5b). Nehemiah said, "Do not grieve, for the joy of the LORD is your strength" (Neh. 8:10b). Sometimes joy seems almost impossible to find, especially considering life's darkest circumstances. In our weakness, Jesus made the way, through His Kingdom, for us to experience His joy. John the Baptist talked about understanding joy just by hearing the voice of Jesus. Later, Jesus explained to His disciples that the love between Him and His Father would facilitate joy for them. He said, "I have told you this so that my joy may be in you and that your joy may be complete. My command is this: Love each other as I have loved you" (John 15:11-12). Love is central to the joy equation, and the only way to really understand love is to know Jesus and the fullness of what He did for us on the cross.

Jesus explained in John 16:20-22 that the disciples would weep and mourn after His death:

I tell you the truth, you will weep and mourn while the world rejoices. You will grieve, but your grief will turn to joy. A woman giving birth to a child has pain because her time has come; but when her baby is born she forgets the anguish because of her joy that a child is born into the world. So with you: Now is your time of grief, but I will see you again and you will rejoice, and no one will take away your joy.

I take special note of the confidence of Jesus here, because he speaks emphatically: "grief *will* turn to joy"! The fullness of joy comes out of the Holy Spirit within us. Jesus promised, "And I will ask the Father, and he will give you another Counselor to be with you forever—the Spirit of truth. The world cannot accept him, because it neither sees him nor knows him. But, you know him, for he lives with you and will be in you" (John 14:16-17). Every prophet of the Old Testament dreamed of that reality, and Jesus specified how that indwelling would become a reality. "The Counselor, the Holy Spirit, whom the Father will send in my name, will teach you all things and will remind you of everything I have said to you" (John 14:26). It's interesting how this goes full circle, because our trust in Jesus opens the door for receiving the gift of the Holy Spirit which, in turn, produces the fruit in our lives. "But the fruit of the Spirit is love, joy, peace, patience, kindness, goodness, faithfulness, gentleness, self-control. Against such there is no law" (Gal. 5:22-23).

It is amazing how the Holy Spirit produces the very nature of the Kingdom of heaven, which is righteousness, peace, and joy.

Words alone do not bring life. Pastor Bill Johnson says it best in the following statement:

> Life does not come from every word that has already been spoken, but by every word that "*proceeds* from the mouth of God" (Matt. 4:4). Notice *proceeds* is present tense. It is the Holy Spirit's breath on the pages of Scripture that brings us into the place of life and purpose.*

---

* Bill Johnson, *Strengthen Yourself in the Lord: How to Release the Hidden Power of God in Your Life* (Shippensburg, PA: Destiny Image Publishers, Inc. 2007) p. 101.

≈ CHAPTER 9 ≈

A TAR HEEL BORN

JASON KENDALL RAY
October 7, 1985 ~ March 26, 2007

With the Blessing of Charlotte and Emmitt Ray

CHARLOTTE AND EMMITT RAY, who were childhood sweethearts, were blessed to be united in marriage later in life. There were three boys already in the mix, Timmy and John Porter, and Allen Ray, II, but God had one more child planned for this couple. The gift of their union was their only son together, Jason Kendall Ray. What a gift. He was wide open! He lived life to the fullest, and he intentionally made every day count. I regret that I never had the opportunity to know Jason personally but feel blessed that I've been given a chance to meet Jason through his amazing parents and the memories before his tragic death, as well as the lasting legacy he left behind because of his decision to be an organ donor. Walk with me through this incredible story of life, death—and life.

Everyone, especially in the Carolina family, knew the story about the Tar Heel mascot, but the CBS special on Jason during the 2008 Final Four Championship series awakened my memory of the tragedy from one year earlier. I was stunned by the life message pouring out of the TV about the Ray family, and I knew that the Holy Spirit was stirring my heart to contact them. I "let it soak" for a few weeks, and I just couldn't get them off my mind. I made contact with Emmitt and Charlotte, and it was clear to me that this was a Kingdom story indeed and that this was a family of faith.

From the very earliest days of his time at First Assembly Christian School in Concord, North Carolina, Jason was exposed to a culture of faith and prayer. Charlotte said, "They prayed for everything there, no matter the circumstances." Jason thought everyone lived a God-centered life with faith, hope, and prayer the essentials of the normal Christian life. It was probably when he was in the second grade that missionaries came to Jason's school to share their adventures around the world proclaiming the "good news" of the Kingdom. Jason was enamored with their work and felt responsible to write letters and stay in touch. He would say, "Mom, guess who's coming to school today?" He was always so excited to hear personally from the missionaries and to have the opportunity to talk with them.

Because they were older when they were married, Emmitt and Charlotte said that they felt the best gift they could possibly give their son was a good, solid Christian upbringing. "If one of us should check out early, he would have the foundation to move forward." One of their neighbors assured them, "Jason got the message!" He truly had a heart for God and was baptized when he was nine or ten. He was forever chasing the deeper things of the faith including the highlight of his summers—camp at Park Springs. On one particular occasion, he called home to ask if he could be baptized again, and of course his parents questioned his motives and whether he had communicated with the counselors that he had already been baptized. He said, "Yeah, but I want to be *sure* that I have things right with God."

Jeff Oakes, Jason's youth pastor and mentor, shared with me that their relationship was special. "My role changed from ministry to mentor. When he moved to college, our relationship grew to a close friendship. Jason had a distinctive flare for the dramatic, a true character. He was larger than life." Jeff said that there were really two important things that defined Jason. "One was that he had this incredible drive to experience life and not just allow life to guide him. He wanted to go for it!! And secondly, he had a real high radar for phonies." He was so intentional with his own pursuit of truth that it made him almost intolerant of people who were hypocritical; he wanted their testimony to be real. He questioned everything! He wanted to know for himself why the Bible had sixty-six books and why those books were the ones chosen. Jeff said it was like a "Curious George streak" that pressed him to understand life. Jason's inquisitive spirit often made him question his own faith walk, but as Jeff explained it, his thirst for truth was the very root of his unwavering and developing faith in the last year of his life. There is no doubt: "He was sold out for the Kingdom!"

Jason's heart for God was not only a concern about his own relationship with Jesus, but he was equally concerned for his friends and especially his family. Emmitt told me a great story that was a typical "Jason moment." They were in the car and Jason, maybe fifteen or sixteen years old, looked over at his dad and said, "Pop, are you going to heaven?" Honestly, Emmitt was offended that his son would ask such a question, and his gut reaction was that he should just backhand him right there. He thought, "I've taken this boy to church all his life and tried my best to reveal the gospel. I simply asked, 'Why would you ask me that question, Jason?'" His son's response was priceless, "I just didn't want to be up there without you, Pop!"

Jason was a deep thinker, and it was apparent that he preferred to keep his personal thoughts close. Charlotte found many journal entries, as early as twelve years old. One topic was: "How do I select my friends?" His main concern was, "Are they a Christian?" Of course, this laid the foundation for his friendships in school. After the eighth grade, he knew he wanted to move to the public school. His parents were very concerned about the bad influences of a secular school, but he convinced them that he would be strong and stand firm in his beliefs. He joined the school marching band and found three guys who later became his closest friends (Chad Hines, Eric Turnblum, and Nick Burns). Robinson High School opened their junior year, and all four of them transferred to the new school. The band they started in high school, "9PM Traffic," flourished. Jason became the unofficial leader, mainly because of his personality and his ability to capture the crowd. The fact that he was the best singer and had the microphone gave him the opportunity to shine. They loved each other, and they dreamed of making it big together! As a matter of fact, this group of young men wrote their own music, recorded their first CD, and had every intention of making rock music history!

Jason was bold, and he lived his faith out loud—not in an offensive way, but in the way that everyone understood that he was for real. He was the life of the party, but he clearly understood where to draw the line with the full intent never to compromise his personal understanding of truth. Emmitt shared another great story he heard from the gentleman helping them produce the fundraising t-shirts for the Jason Kendall Ray Foundation just a few weeks prior to my visit. Mr. Blanford shared Jason's impact on his family in a memory about him and his friend Chad Hines.

Chad was Jason's longtime friend in high school, fellow band member, and roommate at Chapel Hill; they were tight. "I have two daughters, one in Jason's class and one a little younger, and whenever they would ask to go here or there, this party or that, the ultimate test would be one question: will Chad Hines or Jason Ray be there? I knew that if these boys were there, I could trust the situation and the company for my daughters." He knew that he could trust these boys because he had witnessed Jason and Chad both draw the line and make good decisions. They had their limits and would not cross the line or violate their own personal convictions. What a testimony!

After hearing this story, I knew that I had to contact Chad. Like Jason, he said, "I'm an open book!" He seemed pleased to open the pages of this deep friendship. His maturity spoke volumes to me about his own journey, and I marveled at the obvious mutual respect he and Jason had for one another. He talked about the commitment they made their senior year at Carolina, along with Logan Dagley, to have prayer time at the start of each school day, if possible. He said their friendship was very honest and open "and if I felt like he was acting like an idiot, I could tell him. It was cool because it didn't hurt our relationship. It was positive." The most profound comment Chad made during our conversation was that, "In looking back, I see that Jason lived with absolute confidence in his identity. He made no apologies and treated you the same whether he knew you five minutes or five years." Chad is living his life with purpose, and he understands his own identity as well. After the tragedy that claimed the lives of four staff members with Snowbird Wilderness Outfitters, he felt led to work there the following summer. The camp mainly focuses on discipleship training by guiding young people to step into their own spiritual journey finding life and hope.

Jason took the University of North Carolina by storm! As he made his way into his sophomore year, he had the opportunity to try out for the school mascot "Rameses" and never looked back. From the first tryout, Jason *became* Rameses, and for three years he established his place in Carolina cheer history as a Tar Heel icon and a relentless ambassador for the University of North Carolina. His dynamic personality expanded exponentially when he was in the suit! He loved every minute of his time as Rameses, and he took full advantage of the license it gave him to release his passion to the world. In the ESPN story, "Ray of Hope" by Wayne Drehs, Tyler Treadaway, a recent Rameses said, "When you step into that suit, you become this giant cartoon character. But Jason was that way every day—he was born to wear that suit!"* Jason personified the Carolina passion and he was given opportunities to wear the suit at times other than merely UNC sporting events. He understood what it meant to represent the University with passion and pride!!

Jason was also very involved with the campus ministry called InterVarsity Christian Fellowship. That's where he met Isabelle Amaya. She quickly became his "Tuesday night girlfriend." Tuesday

---

* Wayne Drehs, "Ray of Hope," ESPN, http://sports.espn.go.com/espn/eticket/story?page=rayofhope (accessed September 24, 2009).

was the night they met for dinner, planned the InterVarsity meetings, and then worked together to lead the Bible study. He led group leader workshops and often helped with worship. She and thirty other students came to the intensive care ward after Jason's accident.

Jason's senior year, the Carolina basketball program was running on all cylinders, and he was convinced the Tar Heels were going to bring home another National Championship. He actually could have graduated midway through the year, but he wanted to go all the way with the Tar Heels for the title. After winning the ACC Tournament, Carolina looked poised to make a run to the Final Four. The team danced through the early rounds of the field of sixty-four and advanced to the "Sweet Sixteen"! Jason was full throttle with Carolina on his mind.

After the first two Carolina victories, Jason wanted to make time to come home and celebrate his mom's birthday before the trip to New York and the "Sweet Sixteen." He called Charlotte and said, "Mom, I'm going to early church, and I'll be home by the time you get home from church. I'm going to take you out for your birthday!" Well, like any mom would, she decided that just wouldn't do, so she got busy and fixed all of Jason's favorites. She invited other family members, including his big brother, John, and they all had a precious family time right there at home. Jason was pleased. After the big birthday celebration, he left around 2:00 p.m. to pick up his girlfriend, Madison Withrow, for the trip to Chapel Hill.

During my phone conversation with Madison, I came to completely understand the affection Jason had for this amazing young woman. She shared from her heart and started by saying, "Our friendship was all too short!" They met in a mutual class in the fall of 2006, studied together, and just happened to be in New York City together for the New Year. She loved the fact that "he could be ridiculously wild and fun, and then also be very serious." His depth intrigued her spiritually, and she would often just pummel him with questions to discover that passion deep in his soul. She said he personified having life "to the full" idea of John 10:10.

Traveling through this journey of grief, she admitted that through Jason's friendship and tragic death, "It's like innocent blinders were lifted off my eyes, and I was able to see God more clearly. I'm able to see people's brokenness and their need for God. I'm in a completely different place than I was just a year ago." She has discovered the Holy Spirit as Comforter and the "relentless pursuit" of God bringing healing to every area of life.

Knowing that Jason had made the long trip north for the tournament midweek, Emmitt called just to check in. When he answered the phone, Jason told his dad that he was in the Museum of Natural History in the heart of New York City. He was so excited to be there; they had plans for later that evening to go see the Broadway musical *The Producers*. Like any parent would, Emmitt said, "Son, whatever you do, be careful." And Jason answered back with delight, "Dad, I've been here six or seven times; I know exactly what I'm doing!" They laughed, and his dad said, "I love you," and, as usual, Jason's response was, "I love you, too, Pop." That was the last conversation he had with his son.

Jason wanted a snack before the big game. He spoke briefly with his brother John, and Jason mentioned that he was going to take a quick walk to the closest convenience store for a snack. The accident happened around 3:15 Friday afternoon; a car hit Jason from behind. According to the neurologist, Jason never knew what hit him, and he didn't feel a thing. The trauma nurse at the Hackensack University Medical Center found Jason's phone and opened the phone directory. "Dad" was the number she needed, so she made the call around 4:30 p.m. She explained that Jason had been in a bad accident, and it was vital that they get there as quickly as possible. The Rays knew that the situation was critical because of the urgency in her voice. At first, the arrangements to fly north seemed to bog down, but some close friends stepped in, and Randy Marion met them in Statesville, North Carolina, around 8:30 p.m. and flew them to New Jersey. It was a true answer to prayer, and they were standing by Jason's bedside at 11:00 p.m. that night.

In Emmitt's words, "When I saw Jason, I knew that it was fatal. His head was swelling, and he was hooked up to every lifeline imaginable." Jason never improved from the first moments they stood by his bedside, and his vitals were questionable, at best. Over the next forty-eight hours, Jason's parents stayed close, praying for a miracle touch from God.

There is an important idea to remember in any discussion concerning the miraculous hand of God. Charlotte asked me the most difficult question of faith: "Couldn't God have intervened, though, from the devil and brought Jason back?" As we talked about her question, we all agreed that, "Yes, He could have." The only answer I have to why God sometimes brings the miracle and other times He doesn't is that I don't know. The one thing I do know is that God is Good! In spite of the outcome, they quickly agreed! I will never question His ability to bring Kingdom hope into our circumstances. He is able, and, with everything in me, I will always be on the side of contending for the miracle. This is the question that often forces us to go beyond our understanding and just trust Him! The Kingdom of God is different, because the world says, "If I could understand, then I could have faith," but, as Hebrews 11:3 teaches, in the Kingdom, by faith, we understand! It was a vulnerable moment with this amazing couple, but I saw a wonderful glimpse of hope and confidence in our Father.

The Rays continued with Jason's story by explaining how the situation at the hospital progressed. As loving, hopeful parents, they were fragile and tired, and the last thing Emmitt wanted to talk about was possible organ donations. "She was only doing her job," he said, "but the further the discussion went, the more offensive it sounded. It was like we were comparing my son's organs to used automobile parts." He still believed that God was going to touch Jason, so he wasn't going to give an inch. Emmitt finally had to step away from the discussion, and Charlotte met him at the door. He told her what they wanted to do, and he emphatically said, "I'm not going to go through with this!"

As this point in my interview with the Rays, Charlotte interrupted to explain her interchange with Emmitt. She said, "Oh, let me tell you about this conversation I had with Jason, and I haven't thought about it until just now." Jason made it clear that he had made the donor decision himself.

Charlotte explained that when eighteen-year-old Jason showed her his completed driver's license, he was careful to point out something special. She noticed and asked about the little red heart. He said, "Mother, I'm going to be a donor!" His passion dominated the conversation, and he said, "Suppose there was a little child, and their daddy was seriously hurt, and I could save him? If my organs can help someone else, why would I want to take them with me to the grave? They're not going to do me any good! As a matter of fact, I won't be in that grave; I'll be in heaven and have all new organs!"

Jason won, and it was never mentioned again...until the Rays were in that hospital room.

Emmitt was still frustrated and mad. He did not want to talk about it, but he knew that he wanted to honor his son. As he made his way around the corner, he stopped just inside a double door, and suddenly he felt a calming sensation. It was as if the Holy Spirit had released a supernatural peace that he could hardly explain. In that moment, he knew that he was ready and everything was OK. He made his way back to the transplant nurse, Stephanie Falbo, and signed the paperwork. Three neurologists

confirmed the brainwave activity, and the process began for dona-
tion. As they talked with Stephanie about the procedures, Emmitt's
greatest concern was that the team would honor and respect his
son. "I wanted them to treat him like the operation would happen
and then he would get up and go home tomorrow!"

Stephanie embraced their request and promised that she would
be with him every step of the way. Almost instantly, their relationship changed with her, and she became a true ally and trusted
friend. Sanjeev Kaul, M.D., co-chief of the Trauma/Critical
Care and Injury Prevention Section of Emergency Medicine for
Hackensack University Medical Center, said, "There was a great
deal—an extraordinary amount—of sensitivity…We treated
Jason the way we would treat our own families."*

As soon as the donor paperwork was completed, the transplant
process began. Final tests and the required official twenty-
four-hour wait period fueled the progression of Jason's organ
donations. During this waiting period, the potential transplant
recipients were contacted to be on standby. They understand that
this only means they will be notified as to whether they would
actually be having the long-awaited surgery or not later in the
day. Oftentimes, the grueling process begins with the initial call
to the recipient followed by the discovery that this time was a false
alarm.

---

* "A Heart of Gold," Hackensack University Medical Center
2007 Annual Report: A Collection of Caring, (Hackensack, NJ:
Hackensack University Medical Center, 2007) p. 10

David Erving actually experienced the false alarm three times prior to the call on March 26, 2007. Twenty-seven years earlier, the then thirteen-year-old was diagnosed as a severe diabetic. Throughout his teenage years and on into adulthood, David survived many ups and downs with his health. With the serious uncertainties with his blood levels, he found himself in and out of the hospital on a regular basis. After a freak accident in 1997, his broken leg and brittle bone structure clearly indicated the need for a more aggressive treatment, and his only hope for survival was dialysis. After his first evaluation, he was not approved to be on the transplant list. Finally, after several years he made the list.

This late-March call sounded very positive. The invitation to make the trip to the hospital came around ten o'clock Monday evening, and the transplant nurse said, "You have to be here by midnight." Miraculously, he made the deadline, and the doctors came in to explain that the pancreas and kidney were both coming from a young man—very healthy, an athlete. He understood the risk, and there was no hesitation on David's part. The surgery began between 8:30 and 9:00 on the morning of the 27th, and, when the doctors stepped into the waiting room nine hours later, they told his mother, "His kidneys were functioning before we could get him off the table." Success! In one of our earliest conversations, when I asked, "How are you today?", David said, "Terrific!" He couldn't wait to tell me that he is no longer a dialysis patient and that he doesn't take insulin or medication anymore. He said, "I feel so blessed and amazed at Jason's maturity to choose to be a donor at such a young age." It is clear that David is a new man, both physically and spiritually!

Ronald Griffin's situation was similar, yet very different considering the fact that he needed a heart. He started having issues with his heart in 1994, and, by 1999, his condition was fragile, at best. From mid-October 2006, Ronald's condition was critical, and he spent most of the next six months in the hospital. On January 13th, Ronald received a LAVD (Left Ventricular Assist Device). According to the American Heart Association, this device is called "a bridge to transplant."*

There were many uncertainties, and Ronald was on and off the donor list due to strokes, surgeries, and endless medical complications. The very day of Jason's accident, miraculously, he was added back to the list and was actually next in line for a possible transplant. The odds were against him because he was a big man and his blood type was O positive. Jason was a perfect match.

After the successful surgery, his doctor said, "You should become a North Carolina fan!" Ronald laughed and said emphatically, "I did!" It was clear that he was overwhelmed that God chose him to get Jason's heart. He now has a serious side, which allows him to volunteer and share his story of life with other transplant patients. He is a gentle giant of a man who has been given an opportunity to touch others with his sensitive and emotional spirit. Ronald's response to my first question, "How are you today?" was, "Fantastic!" Ah, *life*!

---

* www.americanheart.org/presenter.jhtml?identifier=4599.

Normally, the transplant process is completely confidential, and both the recipient and the donor usually never have the opportunity to communicate about the donor gift, much less have the chance to meet. There has to be mutual assent from both sides for the meeting to happen. Wayne Drehs, the journalist for ESPN who wrote the Emmy award-winning piece, "Ray of Hope," knew that this story needed to be told, and he approached the Ray family. He wondered if they would be willing to meet some of the recipients, and they were intrigued with the opportunity. He convinced them, and, in Emmitt's words, he saw that Wayne was "the real deal" and that they could trust him. Wayne has become a trusted friend and confidant.

As of this writing, over 120 people have benefited from Jason's decision to be a donor. Michael James, the post kidney transplant coordinator for the Comprehensive Transplant Center in Chapel Hill, told me that he was drawn to Jason's story as the recipient list continued to develop. He felt that it was imperative to keep Jason's legacy alive in North Carolina because his accident happened in New Jersey. He also knew that by including the Ray family there would be a better chance to allow Jason's gift to fuel and establish greater awareness of the donor process in our area. Since the initial meeting with the Rays, they have established the Jason Ray Memorial Transplant Fund. Its primary purpose is to provide resources for recipient transplant assistance to help pay the bills at home and enable them to have time to get their feet back on the ground; there is also a Jason Kendall Ray Scholarship Fund.

Emmitt shared a conversation that he and Ronald had after their first meeting. Emmitt said, "He swears that he and Jason talk all the time." Ronald told him, "You've got to be careful when you tell people that because they're liable to be taking me in for psychiatric evaluation!" Ronald told Emmitt that when they were getting ready to meet in New Jersey, he said, "I told Jason that I didn't want to go," and Jason said, "Why?" "I told Jason that I didn't know what to say to them." Then Jason said, "Once you meet Mom and Pop, it'll be all right!" The Rays were astonished with the tone and the words, because one of Jason's key phrases had always been, "It'll be all right!" They saw the message as a gift from God.

Finally, in a recent meeting with the Ray family, Jason's brother Allen called from his home, asking them to bring Ronald over for a short visit. Allen met Ronald at the front door and invited him in, but, strangely, he blocked the way. He said, "Don't take this the wrong way." Allen grabbed the gentle man at the door and gave him a big bear hug. He put his head on Ronald's chest, and looked up with big tears in his eyes and said, "I just had to hear Jason's heart!"

Since the CBS presentation of Jason's life, Charlotte and Emmitt have been invited to share this remarkable story with several church families. The first call came from Lynn Winters, a minister in Arizona, who said, "We see the gospel of the Kingdom in Jason's story, and we would like to honor you at our church." It opened the door for this couple to expand their son's story by making people more aware of the donor process, but more importantly, by giving people hope in the midst of tragedy. This story is a *life* story in the grandest sense of the word and will impact the Kingdom of God for generations to come!

From the very beginning of my journey with the Rays, I keep returning to the movie *Gladiator* and the challenge Maximus made to his men prior to the battle with the Germanians. He said, "Brothers, what we do in life echoes in eternity!" In his short life, Jason Kendall Ray made decisions that have affected people now and will continue to impact the world for eternity. Glory to the King!

CHAPTER 10

GOD IS _GOOD_

Taste and see that the LORD is good; blessed is the man who takes refuge in him.

—Psalm 34:8

For the LORD is good and his love endures forever; his faithfulness continues through all generations.

—Psalm 100:5

You are good, and what you do is good; teach me your decrees.

—Psalm 119:68

The LORD is good, a refuge in times of trouble. He cares for those who trust in him.

—Nahum 1:7

$\mathcal{S}$OME CONSIDER THE WORDS "God is good" a worn-out cliché, but for many of us these words resonate deeply in our souls as truth. How many times have we heard someone say, "God is good," and almost as soon as the words are spoken, the other person answers, "All the time"? The question is, do we really believe these words, or are we just saying them out of habit or reflex? I'm convinced that when we resolve ourselves to this truth in our hearts once and for all, we can find freedom in faith—freedom in the Kingdom—like we've never known before.

THE GOODNESS OF GOD

As I mentioned in the first section of the book, I'm an optimist. I see the glass half full and I see the goodness of God, period. I choose to believe the promises of God, regardless of how farfetched they may sound. If He said it, I believe it! Having said that, my own beliefs and personality traits don't prove anything. Instead of using my words and my experience, I want to use Scripture, because the Word completely establishes the goodness of God!

Psalm 91's promises are eternal treasures:

> He who dwells in the shelter of the Most High will rest in the shadow of the Almighty. I will say of the LORD, "He is my refuge and my fortress, my God, in whom I trust." Surely he will save you from the fowler's snare and from the deadly pestilence. He will cover you with his feathers, and under his wings you will find refuge; his faithfulness will be your shield and rampart. You

will not fear the terror of night, nor the arrow that flies by day, nor the pestilence that stalks in the darkness, nor the plague that destroys at midday. A thousand may fall at your side, ten thousand at your right hand, but it will not come near you. You will only observe with your eyes and see the punishment of the wicked. If you make the Most High your dwelling—even the LORD, who is my refuge—then no harm will befall you, no disaster will come near your tent. For he will command his angels concerning you to guard you in all your ways; they will lift you up in their hands, so that you will not strike your foot against a stone. You will tread upon the lion and the cobra; you will trample the great lion and the serpent. "Because he loves me," says the LORD, "I will rescue him; I will protect him, for he acknowledges my name. He will call upon me, and I will answer him; I will be with him in trouble, I will deliver him and honor him. With long life will I satisfy him and show him my salvation."

In this amazing passage, we find that God is our shelter, He is our refuge, He is our fortress, He is our protector, He is our deliverer, and He is our Salvation! We could camp here for hours, and I challenge everyone to do just that. This passage deserves to be read and reread until it becomes real in our hearts. As we move forward, I want to share how God used this passage of Scripture in my life to prove how *good* He really is!

A year after my oldest daughter's graduation, we decided to do something totally out of our comfort zone for summer vacation in 2006. We rented a houseboat on the Suwannee River. The

Suwannee is a spectacular waterway with miles of uninhabited coastline. Our dockside tutorial lasted, maybe, 10 minutes, and we were on our own. The dark waters and gorgeous shore captivated us as we moved slowly upstream. After a couple of hours, we noticed a storm approaching quickly, and I didn't consider the consequences of continuing our journey. In moments, a storm—a "furious squall"—hit, and the lightning, wind, and rain were upon us. The last thing the owner of the boat said was, "You wreck the boat, you buy the boat!" The girls were screaming, and I was trying my best to keep my wits. The visibility was about twenty yards, and, as I looked to my left, I noticed that the wind was blowing us dangerously close to the shore. My only hope was to gun it and head straight into the wind. It was adventure in the grandest sense of the word.

My youngest daughter is an avid reader, and I yelled, "Bess, get the Bible and read Psalm 91." In seconds, my wife, April, and my two older daughters, Louisa and Amelia, were huddled around Bess as she read and declared this passage of protection over our family. It was an awesome moment! The storm lay down after about forty-five minutes, and everyone was safe. I asked God what that storm was all about, and it's as close as I've ever been to hearing the audible voice of God. He said, "*As you forge these unchartered waters, you are also forging unchartered waters in the days ahead, and I will be with you!*" It took me to my knees, and I knew in a new and personal way that God is *good*!

LESSONS IN SCRIPTURE

John describes the importance of good actions. Listen, "Dear friend, do not imitate what is evil but what is good. Anyone who does what is good is from God. Anyone who does what is evil has not seen God" (3 John 1:11). It is clear here that our actions reveal the qualities of God. Saying this as simply as I know how, God is *good*; satan is evil (or bad)!

"For the LORD God is a sun and shield; the LORD bestows favor and honor; no good thing does he withhold from those whose walk is blameless" (Ps. 84:11). He wants us to have the very best. "God is our refuge and strength, an ever-present help in trouble" (Ps. 46:1). He graciously extends His hand to help us in our day of trouble. God is *good*!

Of course, we have to remember the great passage of refuge, Psalm 23. Most of us can quote it from memory, but do we truly believe the promises of the words penned by the greatest king in the history of the world? God referred to David as "a man after my own heart" (Acts 13:22), and the words written in this short passage, Psalm 23, have been used as a place of comfort for more people than any other words ever written. God is *good*!

Psalm 121 proclaims the protective hand of God. The very maker of heaven and earth watches over us day and night. He will not let our feet slip. He provides shade from the sun by day and the light of the moon by night. He watches over us now and forever. God is *good*!

"For God so loved the world that he gave his one and only Son, that whoever believes in Him shall not perish but have eternal life" (John 3:16). The greatest gift established the hope of the nations and the hope of glory. Jesus explains His purpose later: "The thief comes only to steal and kill and destroy; I have come that they may have life, and have it to the full" (John 10:10). God is *good*!

"The scroll of the prophet was handed to him. Unrolling it, he found the place where it is written: 'The Spirit of the Lord is on me, because he has anointed me to preach good news to the poor. He has sent me to proclaim freedom for the prisoners and recovery of sight for the blind, to release the oppressed'" (Luke 4:17-18). The scroll mentioned in this passage was the prophecy of Isaiah over six hundred years earlier. Just days earlier, Jesus was proclaiming, "Repent, for the Kingdom of heaven is at Hand," and here He uses the words of Isaiah to explain the goodness that will come from His arrival. The blind see, the deaf hear, the lame walk, the dead are raised, and the prisoners are set free. YES! Jesus goes on to explain, "Do not believe me unless I do what my Father does. But if I do it, even though you do not believe me, believe the miracles, that you may know and understand that the Father is in me, and I am in the Father" (John 10:37-38). The miraculous hand of God continues to prove the power of the gospel of the Kingdom. God is *good*!

Jesus is NOT in the grave!

> On the evening of that first day of the week, when the disciples were together, with the doors locked for fear of the Jews, Jesus came and stood among them and said, "Peace be with you!" After he said this, he showed

them his hands and side. The disciples were overjoyed when they saw the Lord. Again Jesus said, "Peace be with you! As the Father has sent me, I am sending you." And with that he breathed on them and said, "Receive the Holy Spirit."

—John 20:19-22

Glory! God is *good*!

After the resurrection of Jesus, He spent forty days with the disciples, and as we have seen, they spoke together about the kingdom of God. "On one occasion, while he was eating with them, he gave them this command: 'Do not leave Jerusalem, but wait for the gift my Father promised, which you have heard me speak about. For John baptized with water, but in a few days you will be baptized with the Holy Spirit'" (Acts 1:4-5). Jesus wanted his disciples to understand that He had made a way for them to live in victory and that His Father was making the way to restore us to our proper place of authority. God is *good*!

"Jesus looked at them and said, 'With man this is *impossible*, but not with God; all things are possible with God" (Mark 10:27, emphasis added). Do we believe it? We each have to decide. Once again, faith is the determining factor. This verse basically says; the impossible becomes possible with God. How awesome! God is *good*!

God's words are compelling and convincing. We could go on for hours, but one final thought concerning the goodness of God must suffice here. God promised Joshua, "I will never leave you nor forsake you" (Josh. 1:5b), and Jesus promised His disciples, "I am with you always, to the very end of the age" (Matt. 28:20b). We must never forget that God is always within reach. "Therefore, I urge you, brothers, in view of God's mercy, to offer your bodies as living sacrifices, holy and pleasing to God—this is your spiritual act of worship" (Rom. 12:1). He wants us to run to Him, to trust Him, to abide with Him, and to praise Him! It's just like a recent prophetic word spoken to me: *"It's not what I do; it's who I am. I am His Son and He loves me, no matter what!"* We have to grasp the fact that He loves us, period. He wants a personal relationship with each of us, and if we are willing to make our bodies living sacrifices, He *will* meet us there, and we will know His will and that He is good.

In order to find healing and true freedom, we must establish the burning conviction deep in our souls that God is good. The enemy wants us to question this truth, in order to keep us in the mire of the hurt from loss, doubt, and disappointment. A rejection of God's truth can empower the adversary to keep us in darkness and imprison us in that cell of disappointment and sorrow.

Trusting as fact the idea that God is good is the path to changing the way we think. The chains of darkness will be broken, and freedom will be ours. In one of his messages broadcast on the Bethel Church podcast, Paul Manwaring says it best: "God is utterly, outrageously *good*!"*

---

* Paul Manwaring, "Kisses from a Good God," (sermon, Redding, CA: Bethel Church, May 4, 2008).

CHAPTER 11

LET THE LITTLE CHILDREN COME

JOSHUA "JOSH" DAVID LANGSTON
August 27, 1991 ~ August 13, 1999

Jesus said, "Let the little children come to me, and do not hinder them, for the kingdom of heaven belongs to such as these."

—Matthew 19:14

With the Blessing of the Langston family

D AVID AND DEBBIE HAD seen several inconsistencies with Joshua's behavior, especially over the previous week. At dinner one evening, David noticed and wondered why only one eye closed when Josh blinked. It was Election Day, early November of 1998, and my wife April saw Debbie at the polls. Knowing that the Langston family home-schooled, she found it odd that Josh wasn't by Debbie's side. "He had a terrible head-ache," Debbie said, and she told April that Joshua was resting in the car with his grandmother. The next morning, David felt the need to call into his office to say, "I'm not going to be in today."

The Langstons have always seemed to be the exemplary Christian couple. Ironically, as we met to review Joshua's story, they emphatically wanted to start with the difficult early days in their marriage—juggling work and family. Dave felt the need to change jobs, mainly to secure their financial future. He was offered a civil engineering position with Dan River Mills. The position provided an increase in his salary but also increased his time at the office. He said, "It was a big mistake, but the Lord used it to teach me later. It took so much time—six days a week, and every holiday. The family suffered, especially my time with Joshua." It was obvious that there was hurt and remorse considering the lost time. Their marriage was suffering, and David realized that a huge wall had developed between Debbie and him. He knew that he had to refocus on their marriage and their family.

The first positive step was a department change at Dan River, and, soon after that, David made arrangements in the spring of 1998 for Debbie and him to attend the "Family Life Marriage Conference" sponsored by Campus Crusade for Christ. This weekend was significant! It refocused their purpose, both personally and spiritually as a couple. They knew that they had to put Jesus first, and they both made the commitment to follow Him completely. In David's words, "The Lord forged great bands of iron around my relationship with my wife, so that no matter what came our way, it would not tear us apart." In short order, this couple found restoration and forgiveness. As they sought and gave forgiveness, the walls and barriers in their marriage crumbled. They were so moved by the ministry of Campus Crusade, the Langstons actually attended a meeting that challenged them to consider joining the staff of the ministry. They started the rigorous application process to work fulltime for Campus Crusade for Christ almost immediately after returning home from the conference.

While considering this new path for his life, David confessed that his home was one of his biggest stumbling blocks. He had designed and built the house on family land, and by being willing to lay this dream aside, he felt that he could move more completely into God's plan and purpose. During the application process for Campus Crusade, they met Martin and Carol Puryear, teachers of Church Based Training International (CBTI). This ministry is designed to equip men and women to study and teach the Word of God and to prepare them for fulltime ministry while maintaining their secular vocation. It looked as though the course would actually begin the first week of November.

Knowing their plans for the CBTI training and their new vision for ministry, the Langstons felt compelled to join the church that they were attending at the time. They made plans to meet with the Elders of the Reidsville Alliance Church in order to share their testimony and join the fellowship. This elder meeting was planned for the first Tuesday of November, Election Day.

Curiously, during the process of establishing the CBTI training and in hindsight, the Langstons had noticed that something wasn't quite right with Joshua. Unknown to them at that time, deep within his brain there was a cell malfunction that duplicated itself and silently a tumor developed on their precious son's brain that would later be diagnosed as a brain stem glioma.

One day while David was preparing for work, Joshua complained of a headache. His dad suggested resting on the sofa, thinking that surely the headache would go away. After arriving home that evening, Debbie had been busy around town with errands, and Joshua had complained consistently throughout the day of a bad headache.

The Langstons wondered if Joshua's symptoms could be some type of spiritual attack and decided to keep the appointment with the elders. They also felt led to take Joshua along to have them pray for his headache. This precious couple confessed their faith and hope in Jesus and the elders prayed for their son.

The next morning, David knew in his heart that he needed to be home that day. After the call to work, he went upstairs and found Joshua lying on the bathroom floor. "He was unable to move or talk or communicate in any way whatsoever." He scooped Joshua up in his arms and asked Debbie to meet them at the emergency room. She then wrapped him in a blanket and handed Josh to David, and he took his son to the hospital. Debbie was overwhelmed with the gravity of the situation, but with great courage and purpose, she systematically called family and friends, especially those who she knew would pray for Joshua. When she reached her dad on the phone, of all the things he could have said after the long silence what she heard was, "We're going to trust the Lord."

As David retold the story, he reluctantly spoke of his first memory of the arrival at the hospital and the meeting with the attending room physician. He led them into the x-ray room where they began to assess Joshua's situation. Joshua was placed in an imaging machine that looked like a big donut, and as the doctor began to assimilate the pictures before him, David could see the big tears begin to stream down the physician's face. He

knew in that moment that something was terribly wrong. Plans were made immediately to transfer Joshua to Brenner Children's Hospital. As David stepped out of the emergency room, he found their pastor George Leibmann and their dear friend Cecil Cottrell waiting there to help in whatever way necessary. David almost fell into their arms, wondering what the future held for his son.

As the magnitude of Joshua's condition became apparent, the E.R. doctor stepped close to David, putting his arms around this dad, saying, "I know it may be hard to believe this, but God is still in control, and He will see you through." Earlier in the year, Dave and Debbie had chosen to believe the sovereignty of God and to stand on the conviction that "God is good." Thankfully, this couple had made a lifetime commitment to the anchor of hope into the gospel of the Kingdom.

As they made their way to Brenner, David found himself planning his son's funeral. In the turmoil, he was overwhelmed with the uncertainty of what to do next. As circumstances would have it, the only thing to do was to take each moment, step by step. He described the first several days of this ordeal as being "beyond imagination." The tumor was pressing on the part of the brain stem that controls breathing, and Joshua was fighting for every breath. Actually, he would stop breathing, for a few moments, and his body would thrash about, and then he would breathe again. As the couple stood by their son, the staff did everything they could to prepare them for the worst.

The medication did not seem to be reducing the swelling of the tumor. Debbie remembers the diligence of one man on staff who worked tirelessly through the night to complete the necessary paperwork for a more aggressive treatment. Before any medical breakthrough, though, David had a sense that God spoke clearly to him early in the morning that it wasn't time for Josh to die. The next morning, David made the transition from comforter to advocate. Miraculously, they agreed to start radiation ahead of schedule, and within a week, Joshua finally found relief.

Over the next six weeks, Joshua made progress through the rehabilitation process. The Ronald McDonald House, located close to the hospital, provided housing for the Langstons during the laborious restoration time. The various types of therapy required daily hospital visits for Joshua, and this provision proved to be a true miracle for their family.

Just before Christmas, the family was able to take Joshua home. His progress improved considerably, but there were many areas of performance that never returned to normal. He was very aware of the situation, and David knew that he and Joshua should talk about his circumstances. As a family, the Langstons had always been forthright, and because of Joshua's spiritual maturity and awareness of eternity, they felt he needed to know. They made their way to a quiet place down by the lake, and David asked, "Joshua, how much do you know about what's going on?" Of course, Joshua had been able to hear the doctors around him during his tests and observations, and he knew something was wrong.

With a smile, David chuckled remembering Joshua's humor, as he responded, "Everybody is treating me like a king!" They shared a laugh and with love and hope, this amazing man of God

explained the journey ahead. He wanted Joshua to know that his time could be limited and if there was something he wanted to do or say, it would be important to verbalize those desires. David marveled at the courage of his seven-year-old son.

After this delicate discussion, it was apparent that this time was very special. This father-to-son meeting transitioned into man-to-man, even, brother-to-brother. There was a tender pause and a time to reflect.

This was a very moving part of my interview with the Langstons. Within moments, we were having an intimate exchange remembering Joshua's improvements and some details about his personality. Around the time of this meeting, physically, he started walking again and actually rode his bike. Debbie said, "He loved to ride his bike; this was probably the pinnacle of his improvement." Unfortunately, he only rode his bike for a few days. Emotionally, he had a true heart for others. Almost at the point of embarrassment, Joshua would ask total strangers if they had asked Jesus into their hearts. Even at such a young age, he was often concerned for others. He loved to laugh and tell jokes. He especially loved his sister, Rachel. In his eyes, she was the greatest gift.

He also had an eye focused on the hand of God. David told one story in his testimony about the removal of a catheter. Several nurses had tried, with no luck, and while they were gone to get a specialist, David and Debbie prayed. David gave it one tug and the catheter came right out. Joshua looked up to say, "Dad, we just saw a miracle," and David agreed, "Son, yes we did."

There were many ups and downs throughout the illness. One particularly difficult event occurred that weekend in February.

Joshua had been doing so well, but he started complaining of extreme headaches. They called the hospital, and the person they talked to said, "Well, he's dying." What a blow! The family and friends all came to say their goodbyes, and finally Debbie took their three-year-old daughter up to the grandparents' for the night. On the drive back, David's dad confessed his concern for their stamina, and the Holy Spirit came and ministered to Debbie as she entered the room with Joshua. She was completely strengthened and encouraged. That night her rest was peaceful and precious. She was awakened with the early morning light and an amazing PEACE filled the room. In that moment, she realized a presence and she witnessed something "like a reflection of fire went across the wall." They both were convinced that an angel had been there ministering to mom and her son. This time, the Lord spoke to Debbie, and she was confident that it still wasn't time for Joshua to die. The next morning, Joshua's main doctor returned from the weekend and called. He explained that fluid was building and was causing pressure on the brain. He asked them to give him a steroid and get to the hospital. Within one hour, the pressure released, and the headaches were gone. Soon after this, it was necessary to add a shunt, and Joshua never had the head pain again.

Once again, Joshua improved, and the family was given more time. There was a lot of daily support from family and friends, and somehow during this hectic time of uncertainty, the family was given a gift of new life. The Langstons were expecting a baby. Paradoxically, Debbie explained that she could have easily died with Joshua and all his pain. On the other hand, though, she knew that her body was responsible for another life. There was excitement and apprehension at the same time, and they weren't sure if another Langston could possibly be a positive thing, considering their circumstances with Joshua. As incredible as it might sound, Joshua was happy for his parents, but he was sad knowing that he might not get to meet the baby.

As Joshua's time grew short, David and Debbie had the presence of mind to call me for information on final arrangements. Their biggest concern was if I could be the one to come to their home to pick up Josh. I was so touched and honored to feel such trust from these dear friends. They were strong and secure with the release of their son. Joshua lived nine and a half months after that Election Day in November, and the Langstons knew that this season had been a gift from heaven.

My family had planned vacation around that time, but I made it clear that I would come home if anything happened. David called early one morning in the latter part of the week. I asked how long it had been, and he said, "It's been a few hours. We wanted to make sure that you had a good night's sleep. The delay is not a problem; we have had a special time with our son, and we want to wait for you." This call was a gift of confidence and a crowning moment in funeral service which I will always cherish.

David described a picture of grace that truly took my breath. He said, "I was blessed with the opportunity of seeing my son live an entire lifespan. We witnessed Joshua grow from a child to an old man. His wisdom increased like that of an old man, and his mobility regressed as well. Unlike a typical seven-year-old, he would sit and ponder." When his mom asked Josh what he was thinking about, he would say things like, "I'm so thankful for the darkness in the night, because you can see the stars shining." Out of darkness comes the Wonderful Light. He also said, "I'm thankful for all of the good times in my life." Debbie said, "Joshua is the perfect example of what the Lord means when He says we have to have a childlike faith." Wow, what a testimony!

The funeral services were designed to celebrate Joshua's life, while intentionally revealing the life of the gospel. David sang and led worship. I was asked to sing "Safely Home" by Jon Mohr, and the words affirmed eternal healing and hope.

> Children, Precious Children, I know you're shaken,
> A loved one taken
>> Oh, but hear Me, Come, draw near Me,
>> Their pain is past now, They rest at last now
> Safely home
> This life is merely shadow, Today there's sorrow,
> But joy tomorrow, Safely home
> They are strong and free, They are safe with me.
> One day you will join them, All together,
> This time forever, Safely home,
> Safely home.*

There is such power in that testimony.

It seemed ironic and comforting that as we reviewed the events, the Langstons revealed the strength they found in God's Word. Even as David described CBTI, he said, "It gives me cold chills." The study was scheduled to begin the first week of November but had been postponed, for obvious reasons, for two weeks. David admitted that this intense Bible study and pursuit of truth carried them through the next nine months of Joshua's illness. In the darkest places, the Light of the world brings *life* while over and over they would proclaim the goodness of God.

Since August 13, 1999, the Langstons have walked through this journey together, all the while seeking first for the Kingdom. As they share their story of loss and disappointment, it *always* leads to life and hope. With a sparkle in their eyes, they share the gift of their children, Rachel, Josiah, Jeremiah, and Jedidiah. Similar to the story of Job, they endured the loss of their first son, but God restored them with three more. As we discussed their sons, David said, "They each have a piece of Joshua. Each one has a unique personality that reminds us of Joshua. What a blessing."

I would like to close this story of restoration with a memory of Joshua. I don't think anything documented here could provide a better description of this little man's heart, so open eyes and hearing ears can find hope in this amazing nugget of truth.

Before his illness, Joshua was a true scavenger of treasure. He lived to find value in all things, from small trinkets to beautiful rocks to significant people in his life. One summer, the Langston children were attending Vacation Bible School. Mrs. Pat, one of Joshua's favorite people, was comparing the story of the value of things to the value of God's gift through Jesus. She mentioned that she had always wanted a large diamond ring and described how valuable it would be. In that moment, Josh knew that he had the solution to her wishes. Some time earlier in one of his "great treasure hunts," Joshua had discovered a giant diamond on the floor of a fabric shop. He was fascinated with this amazing stone. When he explained to the clerk that he found it on the floor, she agreed to let him take the stone home to his treasure box. That stone became his prize possession.

The next morning, he planned to make Mrs. Pat's dream come true. He ran into her class and said, "Mrs. Pat, I've got the treasure that you've always wanted!" Of course, she was grateful for his generosity, but the magnitude of this gift didn't register until his parents discovered what had happened. They understood the value of this stone to Joshua. To him, it was "the pearl of great price!" Without hesitation, he was willing to give his most valuable possession to someone he loved.

I see this analogy as the heart of the Langston family. Joshua was "the pearl of great price" for them, and the *life* that they've found in Jesus and the reality of His Kingdom are offered to us in hopes that we, too, will all find life, hope, and healing.

In the closing moments of our meeting, David spoke of the great truth that resonates throughout Scripture, "What satan intended for evil, God was able to use for good!" He talked about his relationship with the Lord, and he defined their healing with this statement, "When my time comes to go to heaven, I definitely want to see Jesus first, and then He can take me to my son."

CHAPTER 12

DIVINE JUSTICE

OVER AND OVER, I encounter the families whom I serve at various places all around town, sometimes within weeks, sometimes months and even years later. It's apparent that healing is different from one person to the next. Some people seem to be moving through recovery and grief successfully, while others are just getting by. Oftentimes, though, some crumble and never appear to recover. For almost twenty years, I've wrestled with trying to find the common thread that seems to paralyze people in loss.

In January of 2004, Pastor Bill Johnson of Bethel Church in Redding, California, shared his own intimate encounter with loss. One Sunday, he shared a message that he entitled, "Enduring

Faith."* In it, he walked his church family through the horrendous last days of his dad's life and his laborious battle with pancreatic cancer. The following Sunday, which was two days after his dad's death and journey Home, he shared the message entitled, "How to Handle Loss."** These two messages established a benchmark deep in my soul that I knew would eventually lead to an eternal word of life for those facing loss and disappointment. With Pastor Bill's blessing, I include here some of the valuable truths I've learned from his walk through loss and disappointment.

Bill says over and over that he doesn't study to teach, but he studies to experience God more intimately in his own personal walk with Jesus. The messages come out of a practical Kingdom perspective that fuels thousands of listeners around the world to hunger and thirst for more. The Bethel Church community lives in a Kingdom culture that breeds life and the expectation of the miraculous. Bill says that as we move into our own destinies and live out the purpose of God's plans for us, it ignites others to pursue their own journeys with Jesus, which ultimately perpetuates the Kingdom of God.

This chapter is a direct spillover from the ministry of Bill Johnson. As a result of his teaching and encouragement, I have discovered my own destiny and purpose. Along with the two sermons mentioned above, there are two other sermons that God

---

* Bill Johnson, "Enduring Faith," (sermon, Redding, CA: Bethel Church, January 2004).
** Bill Johnson, "How to Handle Loss," (sermon, Redding, CA: Bethel Church, January 2004).

has burned in my heart that need to be spoken in the context of this Kingdom solution to loss: "From Tragedy to Triumph" in April 2007 and "Gaining from Loss" in July 2007.*

We must press in; God is for us, and His healing takes hold as we move forward.

Many of us already know in our heads that God is good, but so many of us have never discovered the full revelation of it in our hearts. My prayer is that we all know more and more, without doubt, that God *is* good! When the crisis comes, though, do we still believe? Do we question God's love or purpose? As people of faith, we often know how to respond biblically to these doubts, but the emotions in our hearts do not always keep up with the beliefs in our minds. Oftentimes, satan takes the questions of doubt and uses disappointment to misguide us into a realm of grief that leads to unbelief and, ultimately, anger towards God.

Based on what he has seen in his travels around the world, Bill states assuredly that over 50 percent of the body of Christ is diseased with disappointment. Even though they verbalize that God is good, when loss or disappointment comes, their trust and confidence in God are shaken. The first question seems to be, "Why did God allow this to happen?" or "Why would God do this?" Even committed believers need to remember: "Hope deferred makes the heart sick" (Prov. 13:12). If satan can deflate hope and trick us to question the goodness of God, he can dislodge

---

* Bill Johnson, "From Tragedy to Triumph," (sermon, Redding, CA: Bethel Church, April 2007) and "Gaining from Loss," (July 2007).

us from the hope that leads to faith. Disappointment is the pain that paralyzes many, including people of faith.

Bethel Church uses different brief statements or phrases that consolidate some of their core values. It helps the church family to clarify purpose and head off distraction. Our family has embraced one of these truths, and it has established motivation and focus for us to believe that God is good all the time. It says this, "We are learning how to feed ourselves on what God *has* done and what He *is* doing, not on what He hasn't done."

One of the greatest failures of many believers is that they tend to feed on what God hasn't done or what He isn't doing, and then they have a tendency to fall into offense towards God, which leads to the ultimate sin, unbelief. Oftentimes being offended at God leads us to be offended at people around us. It then expresses itself as bitterness, anger, and fear. As Pastor Bill was explaining this concept of offense, countless people flashed through my mind that live and grovel in offense. It was as if God was showing me how satan uses death and loss to cripple survivors so that they actually live in death. This is another of the many tools of the enemy used to undermine our potential for refreshed hope and life-restoring healing.

Before any of us were born, God had an idea for His Kingdom, and that idea included us. It doesn't matter how old we are or where we find ourselves in life, He is calling all of us as a people into our divine purpose and destiny. Luke 17:21b is a great reminder: "the kingdom of God is within you." There is no need for distractions to keep us from our divine appointment with His will for us due to an offense.

There is more to say about offense, but we might first be wondering—before considering future destinies—about how to simply deal with this intense pain of loss and disappointment and allow healing and life to return now. Where is redemption and hope?

One thing must be made perfectly clear: it is not a sin to grieve! Matthew 5:4 teaches us, "Blessed are those who mourn, for they will be comforted." Paul also reminds us in Romans 12:15 that we should, "Rejoice with those who rejoice; mourn with those who mourn." It is normal to hurt! God designed and blesses love and relationships, and as the scripture proclaims, Jesus understands our pains, and He meets us in them wherever we are.

There are three key points to note carefully. I believe that they can help us to move redemptively toward healing. First, we can consider King David. He mourned and cried during the illness of his son, and when the word came that the boy was dead, the great king cleaned himself up and worshipped. In spite of the loss, he gave God praise. His servants didn't understand his response. He explained, "While the child was still alive, I fasted and wept. I thought, 'Who knows? The LORD may be gracious to me and let the child live.' But now that he is dead, why should I fast? Can I bring him back again? I will go to him, but he will not return to me" (2 Sam. 12:22-23). There was no doubt or question about the goodness of God. If we are willing to go beyond what we feel and what is convenient, heaven can invade and bring healing to fill in the gaps between what we know and how we feel.

Secondly, we must *never* blame God for the conflict, the disease, the affliction, or the death. Anything that has the appearance of evil *is* evil. I often hear statements like, "God gave me this sickness to make me stronger." No, God doesn't give what He doesn't have. There is *no* cancer in heaven; therefore, God does not *give* cancer to make someone a better Christian or to teach him or her to be stronger! Healing is His ultimate purpose, and He brought the reality of heaven to planet earth so that we could bring it into our circumstances. The Kingdom of heaven *is* at hand, and it is fully equipped to deal with every situation. We must understand that there is no lack on the part of Jesus. The anointing He wants to release is sufficient to overflowing.

All of this leads to the final point and the question that asks, "OK, so where then, is the lack? If it is not with Jesus, it must be with me." We must *not* listen to the lies of the enemy and spin off into guilt and shame! He wants us to say, "Oh, if only I had done that" or "If I hadn't said that." Pastor Bill puts it this way, "The loss becomes a scar. You now have access to a realm of destiny through 'Divine Justice' that you did not have before. You don't have to have the scar, but if you do, use it to your advantage." In other words, our loss gives us opportunity to praise Jesus when we least feel like it. "If you're in the valley, dig a spring, because the lowest point gathers the most water from the outpouring from the mountain."

Usually, in the valley most people lose sight of trust and confidence in the goodness of God. If we are willing to take the blame and slide down that path of guilt and shame, the result will almost certainly be disaster. Guilt and shame only lead to more guilt and shame, and it becomes a vicious cycle of death and disappointment. Satan uses loss and tragedy to infect and poison our trust and confidence in God. Primarily, he tries to get us to question the standard of scripture, which is unbelief, and secondly, he wants to derail us from living in God's ultimate plan and purpose for our lives.

Whatever loss is planted in despair can take root as a seed. Pastor Bill's term, again, is "Divine Justice." It is defined with the example of the word that was given to him after his dad's death. Prior to Mr. Johnson's illness, Bill had proclaimed publicly, and the entire Bethel Church community had embraced the prayer and faith for, a "cancer-free zone." They have had thousands of healing testimonies, many of which have been healings of cancer. They prayed and believed for the miracle for his dad, and it did not come the way they prayed. This outrageous and public attack of the enemy could have caused great distraction and humiliation on this family, but they chose to purpose in their hearts not to let this loss become a source of spiritual disease but one of life and hope. Glory!

Even though this word was a great encouragement, it doesn't change the cost of the seed: his dad. Even considering the cost, Bill stood in front of his congregation and spoke with reckless abandon, "Yes and Amen" to his divine call and purpose. Bill says this emphatically, and I agree, that "you can either sit there the rest of your life and be scarred as a victim, or you can rise with a righteous vindication to see the name of the Lord vindicated."

Before leaving this chapter, we must deal with the stumbling block of offense. The core phrase was mentioned earlier: "We are learning how to feed ourselves on what God *has* done and what He *is* doing, not on what He hasn't done." With this in mind, we may find new insight as we review the familiar story about John the Baptist in Matthew 11.

Jesus spoke with great respect for John. He actually labeled John by saying, "I tell you the truth: Among those born of women there has not risen anyone greater than John the Baptist..." (Matt. 11:11a). In effect, Jesus was saying John was the greatest of all the Old Testament prophets. John was the one to prepare the way of the Lord, and he actually witnessed the Holy Spirit descend on Jesus like a dove: "and a voice came from heaven: 'You are my son, whom I love; with you I am well pleased'" (Mark 1:11).

Later, after he witnessed this amazing vision in the river, John found himself bound in prison. Considering all that John had seen and knowing that God had called him to be the "voice from the wilderness" to call out the Messiah, why would John need to send his disciples to go ask Jesus if He was indeed the one? John knew the job description of the Messiah. He knew that the Promised One was coming to set the prisoner free, but John was still in prison. "Jesus answered and said to them, 'Go and tell John the things which you hear and see: The blind see and the lame walk; the lepers are cleansed and the deaf hear; the dead are raised up and the poor have the gospel preached to them. And blessed is he who is not offended because of Me'" (Matt. 11:4-6, NKJV). John was focusing on what God hadn't done or wasn't doing. Jesus communicated over and over that He only did what His father was doing. Evidently, God had not given the word to release John from prison, and Jesus gently reminded him of the blessing promised for "he that is not offended because of me."

When we feed on the things that God has done and what God is doing, two things happen: we stay encouraged, strong, and focused on what our purpose and life are about, and, as we become strengthened, our focus qualifies us to be a part of the very solution for the thing that concerns us most! If, by faith, we set our hearts on the reality of heaven, we can rest in hope and victory. As Bill Johnson says, "Heaven is filled with absolute trust and confidence in God; earth is filled with absolute mistrust and unbelief, and you and I always reflect the nature of the world we are most aware of."

Pastor Bill, your passionate pursuit of the Kingdom by living in your own destiny and purpose has ignited me to chase life and to share it with anyone who will listen. God Bless You!

CHAPTER 13

THE MIGHT OF A WIDOW

CAPTAIN JAMES RICHARDSON "RICK" PEDDYCORD

August 25, 1967 ~ June 4, 1997

With the Blessing of Marlo Peddycord-Francis

Rick Peddycord's dream assignment came in 1995, and the young couple reported to Hulbert Field, Florida. Rick was assigned to the Air Force's Special Operations Command base where he would pilot the AC-130U Gunship. As described in her book, *The Unkind Companion*, Marlo Francis explained that this particular aircraft had the appearance of a C-130 cargo plane but was laden with the hottest firepower in the Air Force armory.* Over the next couple of years, Rick successfully soared through rigorous training for some of the most delicate and dangerous missions which can be assigned to an Air Force pilot.

Marlo Applewhite Peddycord was, without question, an exemplary military wife. Her courtship and marriage to Rick was one almost like a fairy tale. The first meeting happened in the church parking lot. The Peddycord family's car slid to a stop, just in time to miss the enamored twelve-year-old beauty. Everyone in the parking lot almost had simultaneous heart attacks, while Marlo and the fourteen-year-old Rick Peddycord noticed something more. From that moment, Marlo made it her business to find out more about the handsome young Peddycord. It was apparent that she wasn't the only one glad for the chance meeting! Even after a few years, and his departure to the United States Air Force Academy, Rick's plans for his Christmas break included Marlo. He called ahead to ask her dad for permission to ask her out, and Mr. Applewhite's response was, "You'll have to ask her!"

---

* Marlo Peddycord Francis, *The Unkind Companion: Learning to Live with Loss*, (Mustang, OK: Tate Publishing & Enterprises, LLC, 2007).

Five months after Marlo's first car date with Rick, he proposed, and the couple was married one week following his academy graduation. Over the next eight years, the Peddycords moved twelve times and lived in the fast lane of an Air Force pilot's dream. The adventures were endless, but their greatest adventure as a family was the birth of Benjamin Vance Peddycord in January of 1992. Rick was so proud, and he was completely committed to providing a home filled with life and security for Ben.

Although their marriage was wonderful, from the very beginning of their military journey, Marlo wrestled with a haunting demon of fear. Every success of Rick's career pushed him into a more vulnerable position due to his potential mission assignments. Time after time as he left on each assignment, she wondered what her life would be like if he didn't return. Finally, in January of 1997, as Marlo stood face to face with the darkness of fear, she had one of those "Jesus encounters" that changed her forever. That particular night, she expected Rick to be home from the flight assignment before midnight, and as the clock passed 2:00 a.m., in her words, "the fanged monster of fear returned sinking his fangs deep in my heart." In that moment of desperation, the presence of God invaded her bedroom and the voice of the King spoke: *Do you trust Me?* The comfort of the Holy Spirit disrupted the ploy of the enemy, and this intimate encounter with Jesus destroyed the demon of fear. She was free! Just moments after the fog of fear lifted from her spirit, she heard the keys in the front door. Ah, the peace of God.

On Rick's return from Louisiana and his first full mission as the aircraft commander of the AC-130U Gunship, the Peddycords were scheduled for leave, and the family planned to spend their vacation at home with family and friends. It was a fast and furious departure from Florida, but the young family was thrilled to be going home for rest and refuge. The first two days were spent catching up with the Applewhites and Marlo's extended family while the third day was spent on the farm with the Peddycords.

Another reason that this vacation was so timely was that, less than one year before, Marlo had survived an ectopic pregnancy, and her health had been fragile for several months. The couple was praying for an addition to the family but was cautious about family planning. Marlo's complete recovery was the most important thing. As they settled in at home, Rick and Marlo were pleased to have some private time, hoping that God might see fit for them to have another baby.

Just before dinner, on the third night of their vacation, the family was drawn to a news report highlighting a story in Atlanta about a tragic accident during an air show. Marlo was seated between Rick and his dad on the sectional sofa, and, to their horror, they watched the small plane crash. In her words, "It cartwheeled down the runway like a fireball." The whole family sat in disbelief, and of course those feelings of fear tried to resurface in her mind. Just as quickly as the story passed in front of the screen, Mr. Peddycord said, "I guess it was his time to go," and Rick agreed. This philosophy had almost been a point of contention between her and Rick. She felt that it was almost like they were saying that if our days are numbered, it sort of gives us license to push the envelope (like nothing was going to happen until our days are fulfilled). She had grown up with a healthy respect for safety, while Rick, on the other hand, tended to have a higher tolerance for risk.

As the family caught their breath, Marlo said, "This is bizarre." Pop said, "You know, when it's my time to go, I hope I go just like that." Rick agreed, and Marlo broke the tension and the direction of the conversation by saying, "Would you two just stop! Let's talk about something else."

I think it's important to clarify here that Rick had discovered his love for flight honestly. His dad was an avid airman and actually was one of the founders of the air museum at the airport. He had a hangar and airstrip behind the house, right there on the farm, and from time to time they would keep two or three of the small vintage planes at his hangar. Rick and Pop often spent time together in the sky. The next day, Rick and his dad had plans to do just that. Mr. Peddycord had sold a plane to a gentleman in South Carolina, and Rick would follow his dad, and then they would come home together that afternoon. After their arrival home, the family had planned to rendezvous later that evening at the farm so they could all go out together for dinner.

Rick and Marlo had a precious night together, and the next morning, she was first to make her way downstairs. Rick joined her in just a few moments, and they all had a nice breakfast together. Everyone knew the plans for the day, but Marlo says that she had an uneasy feeling about being away from Rick. She couldn't explain it as anything more than just being anxious. Marlo, Gayle, her mother-in-law, and Jenny, her sister-in-law, followed through on the shopping plans and had a good time together. Marlo and Gayle even talked about the men and their similarities. They were two of a kind and couldn't be happier than being together in the air.

Near the end of the day, they ran into Rick's brother, Jon, and he had talked to Mr. Peddycord after their return from South Carolina. Rick had gone back up to fly a while in the "Bird Dog," a tail dragger. He needed about thirty landings in this particular type of plane for an extra flight job that would help them make a little extra money.

The girls picked up Ben from Marlo's parents, and, as they were making their way home, they noticed that the traffic was terrible. Emergency vehicles were blowing and sounding from all directions. In just moments, Marlo had the worst feeling rise up inside her spirit. It reminded her of that night six months earlier when God had come to her bedside, but, this time, it was different. It was like a supernatural knowing that something was wrong. Gayle had a bag phone, and Marlo used it to call her parents to ask if they had heard anything on the news. In that moment, Marlo spoke, "I feel that this has something to do with us!" Almost simultaneously, her mother and Gayle said, "Marlo, don't say that!" She responded to both of them by saying, "Whatever it is, it's bad, and we just have to pray!"

As we talked, it was apparent to me that even during this dark, uncertain time, Marlo was grounded in her faith and her trust in God. Even ten years later, I could sense the horror of that moment, but I felt a tremendous strength and courage that can only come from the Holy Spirit.

After the grueling journey through the traffic and the arrival to the farm, Marlo was looking for clues. She expected to see one plane in the hangar, and, to their surprise, both planes were gone. An unfamiliar truck was close to the hangar, and, as they were coming to a stop, the truck started moving their way. The neighbor, Gary Edwards, rolled the window down, and his first question was, "Where are Rick and Jim?" Marlo reluctantly responded with, "Why?" As she said this, the margin began to close in. With hesitation, he said, "We were just watching the evening news, and they broke in to say that two small private planes had just crashed south of Asheboro, off of Hwy 42." Then he said, "I just wanted to make sure that they were OK." At that moment, Marlo explained that all of the details were starting to fall into place. The magnitude of the unknown was overwhelming. Gary offered to go find out what he could, and Marlo made her way to Gayle. The two women stumbled into the house, and Gayle stopped in the kitchen, while Marlo ran upstairs to try to get something on the news. She couldn't manage the satellite TV and caught herself staring out the window, looking towards the runway, *hoping...*

Gayle was broken and crying, "What are we going to do?" The kids were petrified. In just a matter of minutes, cars started arriving, and one of the first ones was Jon, Rick's brother. He had no clue at that point about what was happening and immediately went back out to try to get more information. Not long after Jon had left, the final glimpse of hope came for Marlo as her parents drove into the driveway. The power of family is strong, and she knew that if anyone could make things better, it would be Mom and Dad. When she fell into her parents' arms, she knew there was nothing they could do. They were broken for her and stood with their precious daughter to somehow love her through the nightmare.

According to the story in the *Courier-Tribune* following the accident, "Jim Peddycord and his son Rick were killed instantly when the Piper L-4 Grasshopper and Cessna L-19 Bird Dog they were flying touched wings for an instant, veered apart, and crashed in separate fields off N.C. 42 South."

Marlo clearly remembers her own sorrow and pain, but she also communicated her hurt for everyone else. She especially felt an overwhelming hurt for Jon, Rick's brother. In one instant, the men in his life were gone, and he was devastated. Also, friends and family were trying to help with Ben, but, not long after the news was confirmed, little Ben came and crawled up into his mommy's lap. Marlo said that her brain was racing, trying to consider all of the implications of this tragedy for her and her little man. He looked at his mom and asked, point blank, "Is Daddy dead?" and without hesitation, she said, "Yes." Of course, as a five-year-old, he didn't really understand the word *dead*, and his next question was, "Will the ambulance be able to fix him?" Through the help of the Holy Spirit, she replied, "This time the ambulance can't fix

Daddy. He and Pop were hurt too badly, so God took them to heaven to make them well again."[*]

Marlo remembers saying throughout the family visitation and funeral service, "I want to experience the full magnitude of this," and with that decision, she chose not to take any desensitizing drugs for the first forty-eight hours. She didn't condemn it, but, for her, she wasn't willing to give up her connection with Rick or God. She is convinced that the Holy Spirit gave her a divine directive, which allowed her to recall most of the details with amazing clarity. Through the days, weeks, and even months following the horrific tragedy, this amazing widow ran into the arms of God. In her words, life moved on five minutes at the time.

Two weeks after the funeral in Asheboro, Marlo returned to Florida and endured another memorial service at the base for the military family and friends to honor Rick. Within days after the services, she met with a realtor, making plans to move home to her family in Asheboro. The doors opened throughout that process, and the transition happened in short order. Marlo witnessed the sovereignty of God and marveled at His tender hand and grace.

One of the most significant pieces of the equation was that their friendships as a couple remained her friendships, especially Rick's closest friend, Steve Francis. Rick and Steve had established their friendship at the academy together, and their career paths mirrored each other's throughout their growth with the Air Force. They completed pilot training together, and, after making their way through different assignments, they ended up as neighbors in

---

[*] Francis, p. 54.

Florida. Unbeknownst to the Peddycords, as they were finalizing the details on their new home, they discovered the foundation next door belonged to their friend, Steve. As neighbors, their friendship grew even more. They all spent time together with meals and church. Rick, Steve, and little Ben had many great times and made many memories together, just the three of them. Marlo and all the wives of the neighborhood were on the search for the perfect bride for Steve. Rick would encourage him, and Marlo would remind him of the romance yet to come. Steve knew that he wanted to find a godly woman, but Marlo made sure that he didn't give up on the chemistry part. Marlo often joked with him, wondering if this time, "Did you have butterflies?" It was always a resounding, "No!" One night, they were all laughing and Rick went over to his buddy and said, "Steve, one day, God is going to give you a Marlo!"

When tragedy struck, Steve was also crushed with the loss but willingly stepped in to help as a brother and a friend. He actually spoke at both memorial services, honoring his friend and standing as a strong tower for his dear friend's widow. As Marlo described this man of God, "I marveled at his wisdom and strength through this entire ordeal. It was obvious that his actions were laden with absolute truth, integrity, and compassion while all along his motives were completely pure."

The Peddycords were buried on the family farm, and one beautiful afternoon, about six months later, Marlo and Ben spent some time together out on the farm and at the cemetery. On the way home, Ben just spoke out, "I still want that baby brother!" She responded by saying, "I don't think we can work that out," and he was crushed. His next response, of course, was, "Why?" I can imagine her heart breaking as she tried to explain, "Ben, we have to have a daddy to have another baby." He said, "We do," and she said, "He has to be here! I'm so sorry, that's something God would have to work out, but for now, we just can't."

They rode along in silence, and Ben spoke out again by saying, "I want you to get married again." Marlo was shaken by this comment and she blurted out, "You do? Do you know what that means?" Ben explained it without hesitation! He said, "It means you would have a new husband, and I would have a new dad, right? But, I will always love Daddy, and you will always love Daddy, right? Nothing will change that, right?" Of course, Marlo agreed. Then he candidly said, "Well, I don't see what the problem is!"

In that moment, she remembered that precious time when little Ben crawled up in his mommy's lap, and the Holy Spirit reminded her of that prayer that she laid before God, "Lord, seal his heart and let him become all that you've planned him to be." This little guy was speaking life to his mom with Kingdom authority! After another short silence, he looked up at his mom and he spoke his final prophetic word, "I even know who I want you to marry!" At this point Marlo was all ears and he said, "I want you to marry Mr. Steve." In shock, she responded by saying, "Why Mr. Steve?" Without hesitation he said, "Because I love Mr. Steve, and he loves me, and I think he loves you."

Throughout this grieving period and relocation prior to the car ride from the farm that day, Marlo and Steve's contacts had been strictly friendly, genuine give and take, sharing the hurt of their loss. Ironically, several months before the accident, Rick and Marlo were just talking one morning and, out of the blue, Rick said, "You know what? If I was ever shot down in combat and I could have one man watching my back, it would be Steve Francis. I would trust him with my life!" Obviously, looking back, this word of confidence was great comfort.

Marlo made plans to visit her Florida friends some time later, and Steve was in on the plans for the evening. Over the course of the day, things came up, and only the two were left planning to go out for dinner as friends. It seemed a little strange, but they decided to go ahead. The time together was wonderful! They laughed and cried. As they were riding home, Marlo realized that it was the first "good time" she'd had since Rick's death. At one point, she noticed the car was quiet, and she felt a little nervous! She was thinking about the night, and so was he. He broke the silence, and leaning over, he said, "Look at me," and she did, and all he said was, "Butterflies!" She said, "What? I can't give you butterflies!" And he said, "Well, you're doing it!" And immediately she realized that *she had them, too*! When he stopped to drop her off, he walked her to the door, and this man of God took her hands and prayed for God's wisdom and courage and for the Holy Spirit to guide them and lead them. They held each other and cried.

In the weeks and months to come, they carefully opened their hearts to one another. They knew that God approved their relationship, and, some time after a careful courtship, they were married. God has since blessed them with two more beautiful children, Brad and Mary-Marlowe.

The supernatural redemption of God continued on a daily basis. Marlo stood on her confidence in the message of the Kingdom, and her trust that the truth revealed in scripture would be her resting place. As God worked in and through her, He whispered life to her soul. She had ears to hear and knew that out of this horrible darkness, somehow, God had a message of hope that needed to be shared with others walking through their own tragedy and loss. He met this yielded, broken servant in the secret place and the "Dreamed for Me Ministries" was born. Marlo, a gifted communicator and singer, discovered refuge through writing her thoughts, sharing her hurts, and giving life to others.

I've made reference to *The Unkind Companion*, the first book in The Widow's Might Trilogy, an amazing and courageous work describing her journey, facing and enduring her own tragedy. The other titles of the series are *When Casseroles Cease* and *Living It Forward: Stepping into the Light of Your Glorious Future*. The second two books continue sharing her intimate journey through grief and the remarkable, supernatural touch of the Holy Spirit, the Comforter. She has also written a much-needed, four-book series for children entitled *Benny-with-a-Cowlick*. As she watched her own son suffer through the mire of pain, grief, and confusion, she penned this heartfelt work. Her simple and straightforward

approach produces a masterful resource to assist parents and adults with tools appropriate to speak life and hope to children facing tragedy, loss, and disappointment.

I close here with a recent precious story that reveals how the life of the Kingdom continues to guide this family through this maze of healing and restoration. Marlo and Steve prayed about how they would somehow communicate the family history to Brad, their six-year-old. They knew that he needed to be old enough to emotionally understand, and they felt the first "Benny-with-a-Cowlick" book would be the perfect tool to unveil this truth.

Ben was very anxious about the fact that there were two dads in the equation, but his desperate heart cry was that the history would not change his and Brad's brotherhood. Marlo spoke with confidence by saying, "Ben, God did not overlook this detail! God has been so intentional in His plan!" Her faith carried Ben into the meeting, and he knew in his heart that God would be with them as they talked with Brad.

They made plans for a special night. First, Mary-Marlowe stayed with Grandma and Grandpa, and the four of them were to meet for dinner. Brad knew it was going to be a big night! They started in the den. They all agreed that the approach should be positive and they started with, "We are so excited to finally get to tell you some very important news about our family history. As you know, Mommy has been writing books, and tonight I have the children's book for you to read!" He was thrilled and wanted to see.

As the story unfolded, she told him about her special friend, Rick Peddycord, and immediately he said, "That's in your name, Ben!" Ben said, "Yeah, that's in my name." Then Marlo explained, "Our friendship grew and Rick actually asked me to marry him," and Brad blurted out, "Well, you didn't, did you?" And she said, "I did," and with his eyes wide opened he said, "You married him? But you're married to Daddy!" She once again confirmed that she married Rick and Brad said, "What happened; did he die?" From there, this amazing family walked through the story with little Brad, and it clicked! He was moved by the tragedy and thrilled with God's redemptive plan for his mom and dad.

Marlo reminded him of the car ride that she and Ben had from the farm that fall afternoon. She told him how Ben had said that he wanted a baby brother and that he thought she should marry again, and Brad said, "Dad, that's your cue!" Wow! This story unfolded with supernatural grace and fell on hearing ears way beyond his years. As Brad was getting the story, Marlo could still see the anxiety in Ben's eyes. She knew, by faith, that there would be *no* disruption, and she watched with hope and anticipation as she saw Brad hurt for his big brother. The family closed with prayer, but nothing had happened to give Ben the release he needed to know that the brother relationship was okay.

As the family started making their way out of the room, Brad stopped and looked back at his big brother and said, "Thanks for wanting me, Ben!" With the weight of the world lifted off his shoulders, Ben responded, "No problem!" Little men, speaking life.

The family ties were sealed! The Peddycord-Francis family lives to reveal Jesus and His Kingdom. It's a journey, and they plead with us to join them in discovering the redemption and restoration that God has made possible for all.

~ CHAPTER 14 ~

THE MARVELOUS LIGHT

> This is the message we have heard from him and declare to you: God is light; in him there is no darkness at all.
>
> —1 John 1: 5

HOW SIGNIFICANT IS THE message of *light*? The enemy uses loss and disappointment over and over to trap people in gloom and despair. Light will destroy this darkness and illuminate hope and destiny!

I've been a student of Scripture most of my life, but especially after marrying April. I've listened to sermons and studied the Bible consistently for many years, but seven years ago, Shannon

Newsome, a true brother and friend, challenged me to be more disciplined by adding a focused reading plan to my personal pursuit of Jesus. The first year, I read the New Testament. The second year, I read the Old Testament, and then, the third year, I decided to read the whole Bible in a year. Reading the Bible each year stuck, and as I started over again this year, I asked the Holy Spirit to use my reading as more than simply discipline and to allow my daily reading assignments to serve as a channel into the River of Life that flows inside of me.

As I started again in Genesis on January 1, the Holy Spirit spoke volumes! I was blown away with the first five verses, and my 2008 daily reading shook me to the core. I saw and heard powerful truth in a fresh way: "In the beginning God created the heavens and the earth. Now the earth was formless and empty, *darkness* was over the surface of the deep, and the Spirit of God was hovering over the waters. And God said, "Let there be *light*," and there was light. God saw that the light was good, and He separated the light from the darkness. God called the light "day," and the darkness he called "night." And there was evening, and there was morning—the first day" (Gen. 1:1-5, emphasis added). Wow! God's first creative response to emptiness and darkness was *light!* We have to be so careful not to let daily Bible reading be merely a religious act! Have an open heart to *hear* the Holy Spirit.

The Lord made it clear to me that we must deal with the power and truth of the *light* of the world. The depth, breadth, and significance of light lay the foundation on which to build our understanding of the fullness of the Kingdom. When the earth was empty and filled with darkness, God knew that light was the solution. Jesus said, "I have come into the world as a light, so that no one who believes in me should stay in darkness" (John 12:46). Jesus, "The Light," is God's eternal and original plan to establish His heavenly Kingdom here on earth. He was ultimately saying, "By coming to the world as *light*, I am the answer to your emptiness and darkness."

"... the enemy's greatest nightmare is light ..." —Dr. Myles Munroe*

What exactly does Dr. Munroe mean by that? He is applying a powerful biblical truth: "The god of this age has blinded the *minds* of unbelievers, so that they cannot see the light of the gospel of the glory of Christ, who is the image of God" (2 Cor. 4:4, emphasis added). The "god of this age" is satan. Throughout scripture, satan's main objective is to advance the kingdom of darkness. Darkness is ignorance; therefore, the opposite of darkness is light—that is, knowledge. Satan's greatest power is found in what we don't know. Look back at the verse earlier in the paragraph. He blinds the *minds*, not the eyes.

In her book, *The Battlefield of the Mind*, Joyce Meyer sums it up like this:

---

* Dr. Myles Munroe, "Kingdom Series: Contrasting Kindgoms" (sermon, Nassau, Bahamas: The Diplomat Center).

We are engaged in a war. Our enemy is satan. The mind is the battlefield. The devil works diligently to set up strongholds in our mind. He does it through strategy and deceit (through well-laid plans and deliberate deception). He is in no hurry; he takes his time to work out his plan.*

If he can infect our thoughts and cripple us to the point of living in darkness, he will successfully barricade us in a prison of hopelessness and faithlessness. Obviously, without hope and faith, we can never embrace the truth that God planned a definitive destiny and purpose for each of our futures. If we go back to the very first encounter Eve had with the enemy in the garden, we see that satan attacked her knowledge.

> Now the serpent was more crafty than any of the wild animals the LORD God had made. He said to the woman, "Did God really say, 'You must not eat from any tree in the garden'?" The woman said to the serpent, "We may eat fruit from the trees in the garden, but God did say, 'You must not eat fruit from the tree that is in the middle of the garden, and you must not touch it, or you will die.'" "You will not surely die," the serpent said to the woman. "For God knows that when you eat of it your eyes will be opened, and you will be like God, knowing good and evil.
>
> —Genesis 3:1-5

---

* Joyce Meyer, *The Battlefield of the Mind: Winning the Battle in Your Mind*, (Tulsa, OK: Harrison House, Inc., 1995) p. 16.

We do well to notice how he twisted her knowledge by having her question the very heart and purpose of God. As we know from Genesis 1:26, Eve was already "like" God, because He designed her that way. We've been trying to understand the adversary's attack methods for most of human history. Jesus gave us great insight when He described satan as, "not holding to the truth, for there is no truth in him. When he lies, he speaks his native language, for he is a liar and the father of lies" (John 8:44b). He wants us to remain ignorant of the promises that God has laid out in the scriptures.

Often, "Jesus traveled about from one town and village to another, proclaiming the good news of the kingdom of God," and on one occasion he taught them the Parable of the Sower saying, "A farmer went out to sow his seed. As he was scattering the seed, some fell along the path; it was trampled on, and the birds of the air ate it up." Later, "His disciples asked him what this parable meant." He explained, "This is the meaning of the parable: The seed is the word of God. Those along the path are the ones who hear, and then the devil comes and takes away the word from their hearts, so that they may not believe and be saved" (Various verses taken from Luke 8:1-12). Jesus made it very clear that satan does not want us to hear the Word of God. Satan knows that "faith comes from hearing the message, and the message is heard through the word of Christ" (Rom. 10:17). This verse is in *present* tense. It doesn't say having *heard*. Hearing releases faith, and faith destroys the work of the devil.

The enemy understands that if he can keep us from the Light (the Word), he can deceive us to live in darkness. When it comes to loss, darkness often leads us to camp in that place of disappointment and offense. It then imprisons us, and we can only move from disappointment to disappointment or from offense to offense. This prison disrupts everything that looks like life or hope and whether we verbalize it or not, we wonder, "Is God really good?"

Jesus came into the world as the Light so that disappointment and offense can be broken, once and for all. God is *good*! God's ultimate design goes beyond Jesus coming as the Light of the world. He planned it so that, through Jesus, *we* can become that very *light*! Jesus came as the Light, and then, by the supernatural design of God, now we are the *light*! "For you were once darkness, but now you are light in the Lord. Live as children of light" (Eph. 5: 8).

Paul said, "You are all sons of the light and sons of the day. We do not belong to the night or to the darkness" (1 Thess. 5:5). God's power makes a reality of an incredible claim: "As He [Jesus] is, so *are* we in this world" (1 John 4:17, NKJV, emphasis added). That means that we actually become the *light* of the world. That's why Jesus said, "You are the light of the world" (Matt. 5:14a).

Glory!

By God's grace and sovereign will, *we* are the *light* of the world! We won't be, though, if we don't accept this fact with ears to hear and believe it! Faith comes from *hearing*!

Satan will do whatever it takes to keep us from knowing this dynamic truth. He is so afraid of the light that he often tries to use it to his own advantage. "And no wonder, for satan himself masquerades as an angel of light" (2 Cor. 11:14). So, how do we determine the true light from the false light? There's an amazing passage in Romans that explains what we must do to withstand the threats of the enemy. It says, "And be not conformed to this world...."

In other words, we do not have to listen to the god of this age! He is a liar and wants to keep us in darkness, "but be ye transformed by the renewing of your mind, that ye may prove what is that good, and acceptable, and perfect, will of God" (Rom. 12:2 KJV). In a renewed mind, faith will grow, and the light will destroy the darkness. The Kingdom of God will live inside of us, and the reality of heaven will invade every area of our lives.

With everything in me, I want everyone to realize what happens when we accept Jesus as King. We're not just offered some "fire insurance" which includes a free ticket to heaven. When we *become* His sons and daughters, our transformation is immediate. His life and light are for right *now* (even as we grow and mature from that point on)! When we receive forgiveness, we are reclaimed and adopted into God's family *forever*—and right now! In Christ's Kingdom, we *become* the Righteousness of God! We *are* the *light* of the world! The Kingdom of God is *within* us! We *are* a divine encounter! God has a plan and purpose for us! Most importantly, God, the maker of the universe, *loves us*!

As I write these words, I know that God wants to reach into broken hearts and set them free. God did not say to arise and reflect the light, No! He said, "Arise, Shine!" Isaiah prophesied these words hundreds of years ago, but I believe in my heart that God has this very word for us today!

> Arise, shine, for your light has come, and the glory of the LORD rises upon you. See, darkness covers the earth and thick darkness is over the peoples, but the LORD rises upon you and his glory appears over you. Nations will come to your light, and kings to the brightness of your dawn. Lift up your eyes and look about you: All assemble and come to you; your sons come from afar, and your daughters are carried on the arm. Then you will look and be radiant; your heart will throb and swell with joy....
>
> —Isaiah 60:1-5

We are meant to experience this blessing for ourselves in all of our todays: "if we walk in the light, as he is in the light, we have fellowship with one another, and the blood of Jesus, his Son, purifies us from all sin" (1 John 1: 7). Why shouldn't we take a chance to walk in the *light?* What do we have to lose? What might we gain? We might actually find life like never before. In my life, intimacy with God has changed me forever, and I found the heart of the light wrapped up in the words to the Charlie Hall song, "Marvelous Light":

The Marvelous Light

I once was fatherless, a stranger with no hope
Your kindness wakened me, wakened me from my sleep
Your love it beckons deeply, a call to come and die
By grace now I will come and take this life, take Your life
Sin has lost its power, death has lost its sting
From the grave You've risen…victoriously!
Into marvelous light I'm running
Out of darkness, out of shame, by the cross
You are the truth, You are the life, You are the way
My dead heart now is beating, my deepest stains now clean
Your breath fills up my lungs, now I'm free, now I'm free
My dead heart now is beating, my deepest stains now clean
Your breath fills up my lungs, now I'm free, now I'm free
Lift my hands and spin around, see the light that I have
    found
O the marvelous light, marvelous light*

Jesus stands with His arms open wide, living in victory and leading in hopefulness and loving us with "healing in His wings." The sun of righteousness** is risen and is standing ready and always able to set us free and reveal His *marvelous light*—in His word, in this world, and in our hearts, our minds, and our daily circumstances. May that be for each of us, by His powerful grace, the life story we have to tell!

---

* Words and music by Charlie Hall © 2004 Generation Music.
** See Malachi 4:2

Closing Thoughts and Prayers for Hope and Healing

EVERYONE FACES LOSS AND disappointment, but Jesus is calling us to "change the way we think, because His Kingdom is within reach!" It is fully equipped, by the Holy Spirit, to establish righteousness, peace, and joy in our lives—right now. He wants us to be free, and He wants us to know that we have hope and a future. He did not die on the cross for us to merely go to heaven (though it doesn't get much better than that!). He came that we might have *life*, here on earth and to have it to the fullest!

Dear Lord, wrap Your amazing arms of power and grace around the hurting ones in special need of Your healing. As they embrace the truth of your Kingdom, Jesus, let Your Holy Spirit become a river that expands to overflowing. Let them know that they are Your sons and daughters and that You have healing, hope, and a future for them, starting right now. Reveal that light, Lord, and let darkness be destroyed forever!

Father, I pray that the reality of heaven would invade their circumstances in every way, and that the authentic, supernatural gospel of power and authority would be established in every aspect of every journey made with You.

I praise You, Jesus, and thank You for giving me the opportunity to share my story, along with the stories of these other amazing Kingdom families so others may live! In Your precious name. Hallelujah! Amen.

REFERENCES

Angelou, Maya. Quoted in Avaneda D. Hobbs, *Dr. Maya Angelou: As Seen Through the Eyes of America (Honoring a Woman Full of Life)*, Forestville, Maryland: CAP Publishing & Literary Co. LLC, 1999.

Eldredge, John. *Epic: The Story God Is Telling*. Nashville: Thomas Nelson, Inc., 2004.

Eldredge, John. *Wild at Heart: Discovering the Secret of a Man's Soul*. Nashville: Thomas Nelson, Inc., 2001.

Foster, Kyle. "A Football School Mourns." Fayetteville: *Fayetteville Observer*, September 10, 2000.

Francis, Marlo Peddycord. *The Unkind Companion: Learning to Live with Loss*. Mustang, OK: Tate Publishing & Enterprises, LLC, 2007.

Fullam, Dr. Terry. "Life on Wings." Sermon, Holy Spirit Conference, November 10-12, 1989.

Drehs, Wayne. "Ray of Hope." http://sports.espn.go.com/espn/eticket/story?page=rayofhope.

"A Heart of Gold." Hackensack University Medical Center 2007Annual Report: A Collection of Caring. Hackensack, NJ: Hackensack University Medical Center, 2007.

Johnson, Bill. "Enduring Faith." Sermon, Redding, CA: Bethel Church, January 2004.

Johnson, Bill. "From Tragedy to Triumph." Sermon, Redding, CA: Bethel Church, April 2007.

Johnson, Bill. "Gaining from Loss." Sermon, Redding, CA: Bethel Church, July 2007.

Johnson, Bill. "How to Handle Loss." Sermon, Redding, CA: Bethel Church, January 2004.

Johnson, Bill. *Strengthen Yourself in the Lord: How to Release the Hidden Power of God in Your Life.* Shippensburg, PA: Destiny Image Publishers, Inc., 2007.

Johnson, Bill. "The Nature of Faith." Sermon, Redding, CA: Bethel Church.

Manwaring, Paul. "Kisses from a Good God." Sermon, Redding, CA: Bethel Church, May 4, 2008.

Meyer, Joyce. *Battlefield of the Mind: Winning the Battle in Your Mind.* Tulsa, OK: Harrison House, Inc., 1995.

Monroe, Dr. Myles. "Kingdom Series: Contrasting Kingdoms." Sermon, Nassau, Bahamas: The Diplomat Center.

Tolkien, J.R.R., *The Fellowship of the Ring.* 1954.

USAF Pararescue. Pararescue motto written by Lt. Col. Richard T. Kight and originally titled "The Code of the Air Rescueman." Can be found in AFDD 2-1.6 Personnel Recovery and at http://www.pararescue.com.

RECOMMENDED READING

Rediscovering the Kingdom, Dr. Myles Munroe

Strengthen Yourself in the Lord: How to Release the Hidden Power of God in Your Life, Bill Johnson

The Supernatural Power of a Transformed Mind: Access to a Life of Miracles, Bill Johnson

The Supernatural Ways of Royalty: Discovering Your Rights and Privileges of Being a Son or Daughter of God, Bill Johnson & Kris Vallotton

When Heaven Invades Earth, Bill Johnson

The Widow's Might Series: The Unkind Companion; When Casseroles Cease; Living It Forward Marlo Peddycord Francis

Wild at Heart: Discovering the Secret of a Man's Soul, John Eldredge

IF YOU'RE A FAN OF THIS BOOK, PLEASE TELL OTHERS...

- Write about *Life Stories* on your blog, Twitter, Myspace, or Facebook page.
- Suggest *Life Stories* to friends.
- When you're in a bookstore, ask them if they carry the book and if not, suggest that they order it.
- Write a review of *Life Stories* on amazon. com.
- Email suggestions on other websites, conferences and events you know of where *Life Stories* could be offered.
- Purchase additional copies to give away as gifts.

CONNECT WITH ME...

If you'd like to learn more about *Life Stories*, check out my website at **www.lifestories.cc**.